THE OTHER WOMAN

Helping To Protect Young Women
From Narcissist Married Men

Based On A True Story

Jacqueline Servantess

DISCLAIMER

This book is based on a true story and my hope would be to share with 100% accuracy from what has taken place, and to share useful information that would be of encouragement and support. That being said, and also with regards to what's been termed as human error- which is something I of course cannot control... I don't claim that everything in this book is for sure 100% accurate, or that I might not re-read something later on and feel "oh I should have edited that out" or "oh I should have written that differently," etc. Also, as this book is meant to share information about true life experiences that did happen- for legal and privacy purposes, I have intentionally changed the names of those involved.

It would truly be my great hope for every reader to be able to take much good from this book, and for the book's content to be used to help and benefit many..! Additionally- I do share everything as a student not a teacher and cannot be responsible for anyone's choices, or the outcome of those choices. With regards to anything that would require a government-approved professional, whether medical, psychological, spiritual, or anything else- that is not territory I would venture into what so ever and so all readers would be required to have that government-approved oversight please with regards to any of those types of things, as well as anything else that may be relevant... Thank you!

There are two acknowledgements I would like to please be sure to include here. The first one that I must of course include, is to my blessed Creator Y-HWEH. I believe He has been with me through every moment of my existence and has continued to love me and have good plans for me, even when I was not making decisions that pleased Him! He is Love. He is faithful. He is patient, and He is forgiving! And I believe that mankind means so much to Him! All anyone would need to do, would be to commit themselves to Him, our Messiah Y-HWEH Y-hoshua Jesus Christ, 100%, in faith..!!! Next, there is an exceptional person that I would like to acknowledge, and that is my late grandmother Judith. I only knew her as a young child, as I believe she was tragically one of the many victims of a corrupt medical system- but she was an incredibly special woman and I believe that if she were here today, she'd be one of my biggest supporters and best friends!

"For God Y-H so loved the world that He sent His only begotten Son that whosoever believes in Him should not perish but have eternal life."

JOHN 3:16, THE HOLY BIBLE

CONTENTS

COMING SOON

I've created a free GIFT for my readers that is available NOW and has one of my #1 tips in helping to *discern if he's a narc **from the start**!*

So, I invite you to take a quick moment right now and go to www.jacquelineservantess.com/from-the-start and enter your email address, and I'll send you your free copy without delay!

PREFACE

My name is Jacqueline and I'm what you might call, a Torah-Keeping Truther, Prophetess-in-training. I have a ministry-focused youtube channel, numerous passions, and have worked very hard to get to where I am today.

Despite a shockingly traumatic childhood, into an early adulthood that left me at the age of 24, feeling forced to rely on God to rescue my life from challenges clearly only He could get me through- and despite not being 100% clear of Who He was- I determined to begin to pray every morning and night, and turn to Him for help. It was not long later, at the age of 25 that I believe I was led from Above to decide to try believing in The LORD Y-HWEH Jesus Christ, and was born-again.

There was still going to be a lot to persevere through- but nothing could ever compare to the hardship of what it was like for me prior to having found Him. It's now been over a decade since becoming a Believer in The LORD Y-HWEH Jesus Christ, and I'm so thankful to report that *a lot* of amazing things have happened. To briefly mention one of them, as it relates to this book- it seems I've very often received dreams that I believe have been from Above- and I've even been shown in a dream to write this very book, title included..!

I should perhaps clarify that I, of course, don't believe all dreams are from Above, by any means, and that I'm a huge supporter of patiently and diligently continuing in prayer and in reading from The Holy Bible (His Word), which I believe may both be very important and helpful practices in helping to discern truth. Additionally, I am a huge promoter of not only reading but also obeying His Word, which I do believe is a way to help mankind express our love for Him, and also supports us in our own stability.

I believe that The God of The Bible is Love and that even part of the reason, if not the entire reason, that I was shown to write this book, is because of His love for mankind…!!! I'd ended up having multiple dreams on the topic, and something I was shown, went maybe something like this: I was to write this book and share about an experience I'd had several years ago with a married man who was a narcissist; and that the intention of this book was to try to help protect young women from such types of individuals.

Some of the things I think I may have specifically been shown to include in the book, maybe went something like: that regarding such men- if they would be willing to be unfaithful to their wives in the first place, they would also typically be willing to eventually turn around and be unfaithful to the young woman they might have ended up with. Also, that these types of men would typically seek to regularly have one or more women in the background somewhere, lined up and ready for them to be able to eventually try to pursue. I think I may have also been shown that while these types of men had perhaps portrayed a very convincing story to the young women that they were targeting, about how awful their wife was, etc.- that the story they'd told was untruthful and deceptive, and highly manipulative.

As for me, I count it an honor and a privilege to have gotten to a place where I'm able to take from experiences I've encountered and information I've learned, that relate to the topics at hand, and am so thankful to Y-H for the huge blessing of getting to see it being used for good; and not only for myself- but also for the good of others that I might be able to be of service towards.

And so, as my story does stand, I am not able to testify that at certain points in my walk as a Believer, things didn't get messy, and that I never had any major slip-ups. But, what I can state is that even despite those things, as well as the possible severe discipline that I've also faced with regards to them, I believe that God is gracious and that His discipline actually has helped to show all the more that He cares..!

For whom Y-HWEH loveth He correcteth; even as
a father the son in whom he delighteth.

Proverbs 3:12 KJV-ED

Thanks be to The One True God Y-H for His continued grace and forgiveness, and that even my past major slip-ups have been used for my good. I believe that apart from God, we can do nothing, so if there's any good in anything I do on this earth, may He be glorified. In The Name and by the blood of The LORD Y-HWEH Jesus Christ, Y-hoshua Ha'Mashiach, ahmen.

INTRODUCTION

I should maybe share a bit more background before going forward... Pretty much, I grew up in a Jewish community and after my parents got divorced when I was 7 and my dad's company fell apart, we moved to a community that was not exclusively Jewish and I began attending a public elementary school. I was shocked to see a whole other world out there and the truth is... I liked it! Eventually we moved again- this time to USA- and it was there that I was really exposed to even more of a different culture.
I remember in 5th grade being told that wearing all blue was not a good idea because gangs downtown might jump someone for that! I also remember somehow being left unsupervised at a park and getting into a conversation near the bathrooms with some nazi type of street people, who eventually asked about if I was Jewish, and that was the first time I heard a discriminatory word I will not repeat.

I think, since arriving in USA, that there may have also been some other anti-Jewish comments I'd heard along the way- maybe even through the media- and so the result was that I ended up for maybe almost 2 decades, not wanting my peers to know I was Jewish because I thought they might think negatively about me, sort of thing!

All that being said, it was when I was around 12 years old, that I believe I felt God "call me." I remember where I was, and I remember my response. I felt like He wanted to try to use me to make some type of positive difference and my response was maybe something like "look how much corruption is out there! How vast it is! All the way up to a white house level! So what can I do? I'm just one young girl! I'm just going to focus on myself, go to college, and do my thing..."

To that point in my life I had been through some pretty significant trauma, but I was also very resilient and so it didn't hold me back from being the upbeat, caring, and straight A student that I was. That being said, being "called by God" was something that was so different from what "the world" portrays as even being a possibility... And no less, as a female, who was only around 12 years old.

So, the way I see it is that I tried to say no, but God had other plans. I believe it was after that point that a lot of extremely difficult hardship came my way and this time it was too much for me to bear. I was broken down and destroyed in many ways. There's a lot that happened and I won't go into all the details in this book but I finally did find myself deeply traumatized and in a pretty desperate place. On a positive note, after going through some of the things that I did, I did develop a very strong determination to try to seek justice for the oppressed and make a difference.

But the thing is that I was extremely broken and didn't really know what to do about it. I got to a place where I knew I needed to go forward but I also knew I didn't have the strength. And that is when I finally by God's grace decided that I would begin to pray every day, morning and night. I would literally just lie in bed and pray my own prayers... and that's what I did.

I had ideas about Who God was, at that time, that were not correct- but I believe in His love and goodness, He saw that I was seeking The One True Creator, and He heard me and attended to me. I had 3 "to do lists" and was very burdened, but I found after I had begun my daily prayer, that things started to get done and He was giving me that strength that I needed to do what I needed to do.

Hallelu Y-H.

I did decide to try believing in The LORD Jesus Christ around Passover 2010. I didn't know for sure if it was "the right path" but I decided to try it, and I was sincere. And pretty much, I became like a totally different person the next day! I didn't know that when a person gave their life to Him they were to become "born again" and receive Holy Spirit and their desires would change. But that's exactly what happened! I believe it was that very 1st day, that I said "I don't know what it means, and I don't know if this makes any sense, but I feel like I need to be baptized! I don't even know what that is?!" And so I looked in The Bible and I saw that I was right- over and over again I found that after people gave their lives to Messiah, they were baptized. I said "I don't know how I knew that but I"m right I need to be baptized!" Months later after continuing to read The Bible, I learned that the reason I knew that (and so much more!) was because I had received Holy Spirit and one of the things He does is teach us!

So, I was a very perceptive and discerning person and most definitely street smart as well... But the one main "blind spot" that I had, was regarding abusive men. Because of the abuse I'd endured growing up, I had been "trained," in a sense, to accept that type of behavior and had even, unknowingly, developed what's commonly called codependence. I'll get into the topic of codependence later in this book, but just to please be clear from the beginning- codependence is not necessarily as it sounds, and many extremely independent people may actually face challenges with regards to it!

So, that being said, and especially without a strong support system around me, I did find myself continually targeted by those types of individuals. And despite how insightful I was, and all the knowledge and discernment I had developed, even after giving my life to Messiah... when it came to relationships and the deep desire to feel "loved"... there were still some things that needed to be worked out.

Since being born-again, it's been an incredible journey and God has shown me much favor. After around a year I did realize I needed "deliverance" and did seek that out, and that was really a turning point in my life, as well! And despite having already gone through a lot of inner-healing, it was really in approximately 2017 that I believe God allowed me to come across some really cutting edge information, that helped me take things to a whole new level with regards to releasing any and all pain that may have still been inside of me! It is also around that time that I finally learned what NPD was and it helped really put the puzzle pieces together between things I knew about so well based on the experiences of being around such individuals- and that actual science behind it. It was also around that time, that I was shown to write this book.

And so, as far as this book is concerned, I hope to help shine light on this serious topic that has affected many young women and needs to be addressed and exposed. These influential, often older, married men with a serious personality disorder called Narcissistic Personality Disorder (NPD), who have continually manipulated and preyed on these women who just didn't see it coming! Maybe the women had certain weaknesses to deceptive men due to something in their history- or maybe not! Either way, women need to be armed with the knowledge about what NPD is and how to identify the warning signs from the very beginning.

And so while I do feel terrible for the poor decisions I made when I was newer to the faith, and before I even recall knowing what NPD was, and while I am potentially still paying a price for the missteps I made until this very day- at the same time- I was also very very much a victim and I hope that please remains 100% clear and stood by! And to please also clarify: having been a victim to a cunning and deceptive narcissist isn't something to identify in order to mope in it and embrace "victimhood" as a title to live by, by any means! The purpose for identifying having been a victim is to see the situation for what it was, in order to help support the individual in determining what the next steps should be in order to continue forward, and see what happened be used for good in their life! From "victimhood" unto being an "overcomer." That's what it's about!

Thank you!

CHAPTER 1: MEETING THE NARCISSIST

Sitting on some steps on a platform outside, it was another beautiful day in Jerusalem, Israel. It was the year 2014, and things in Israel were quite peaceful around that time, so to speak... Unlike other times in history- including even since then- with regards to islamic violence- there wasn't a sense of fear to go outdoors, and people weren't hesitating to live out their days "as usual."

I had spent most of my life growing up in Canada, but had moved to Israel in 2012, believing it was something I was being led from Above to do. I'd ended up living there for about 4 years, and though that is quite a while, in many ways I was not able to settle down there during that time, whatsoever. A main reason for that, was that I had been facing a long and drawn out process in seeking my right to Israeli citizenship. Even though there was a law in place to protect Jewish rights to that citizenship, there was also discrimination against Jews who believed in The LORD Y-HWEH Jesus Christ. Well the fight went on, and after about 3 years when violence did pick up for a while in Jerusalem, I decided to move to Southern Israel where I thought things might be more peaceful...

That was actually after the major mis-step with the narcissist had taken place, and after I'd repented of it. However, I do question to this day, regarding- if I had never made that mis-step with the narcissist- if a lot of the things that followed would never have happened either. If I would have recognized that I was not meant to leave Jerusalem, and if I also would have finally won that case that I'd been fighting all those years. But that is not what happened... I did leave Jerusalem on my own accord, despite it not being what Elohim God had shown me to do, I don't believe... And I did also end up losing that case I'd been fighting all that time!

Of course, I do also believe that Elohim God knew that I was going to make that mis-step with the narcissist before I made it, and before I even stepped foot in Israel to seek citizenship. That He knew that would happen, as well, as what would happen thereafter. And so in a way, I do feel that they were lessons I was going to be meant to learn- as regrettable as those choices were... And they were lessons I was going to be learning the hard way. One of the things I hope to be accomplished with this book is that it will help protect other women from learning things the hard way and from being deceived by cunning narc men in the 1st place!

I firmly believe in and stand by the fact that all humans have free will, and I also at the same time stand by the fact that God Y-H knows exactly what everyone is going to do, before they do it. It's just for us to experience it for ourselves. So, while I did learn a lot the hard way, the fact is that I have learned, I have grown, and it has been used for my good.

So, after having one of the hardest years of my life once in the South, and the result in court not being as I'd hoped.. it seemed to me that it was time to take a break from fighting things out in court- at least for a season- and return "home" to Canada. That being said, I do not regret going to Israel, what so ever, and do still believe 100% that I had been meant to go there, without question. I feel that, as someone who'd never actually even visited Israel prior to those 4 years, it was a very valuable experience for me and helped me gain a much clearer perspective about Israel's politics and culture, and even helped me to understand myself better as a Jew. While I did leave Jerusalem for that last year or so, I'd spent most of my time in Israel living in Jerusalem, which I feel is truly "my city," so to speak.

The Presentation

So, back to the account... It was in 2014- I was a somewhat "new" Believer, and about halfway through my time in Israel. I was sitting by those steps in that public space in Jerusalem, reading from The Word of God and minding my own business, when seemingly "out of nowhere" a somewhat older Spanish man- maybe in his early 50's- interrupted me. He started speaking to me, and actually ended up coming quite close up to where I was sitting.. In fact, I believe he eventually ended up coming down to my level, by bending both of his knees, and in the meantime, leaving his friend standing off quite a bit more to the side. After a bit of short dialogue, he ended up speaking to me about Jesus Christ, and my response was perhaps something like- "I know He's The Messiah; yes I'm a Believer as well."

I think he and his friend both may have been pretty surprised by my response. For the most part, I did generally dress similarly to the orthodox Jews.. I would either wear a dress or skirt and it may also be quite long.. and so, it was just quite obvious that I was a Jew. That being said, most people would likely not have guessed based on briefly seeing me, that I was actually a Jewish Believer in The LORD Jesus Christ. The thing was, though, that those men were also dressed similarly to orthodox Jews, so I wouldn't have guessed, either, that they would also end up portraying themselves to be Believers in The LORD Jesus Christ.

On the topic of Believers- I believe there are 3 main groups of Believers. There's more of the mainstream Christian group (as the largest in size), there's more of the Messianic and traditional type of group (as medium in size), and then there's more of the Torah-Keeping group (as the smallest in size).. But despite the 3 different community's numerous differences- for those of us who are sincere, etc. and have been born-again- I believe that we are all brothers and sisters in Christ Messiah, and that there is a degree of unity between us, regardless of our differences.

So while I, personally, was more from the smallest Torah-Keeping group, and I believe that those men may have portrayed themselves to identify more closely with the medium-sized Messianic type of group- especially as those two particular groups were so few in number, and both shared a degree of common interest in "Jewish things"- randomly meeting each other was something that seemed somewhat out of the ordinary...

But... people aren't always who they portray themselves to be. And being alone in Jerusalem without much community in my life at the time, added more reason for the wrong type of person to want to try to target me... Despite being quite "street smart" and also being quite good at sensing how to keep myself physically safe- I was still a bit susceptible to being conned emotionally... I'd been through so much in my life and despite having already overcome and worked through so much, there was a part of me that was seemingly starving for love and approval. That, of course, would not justify wrongdoing on my part, but I do think those facts are still important in helping to provide relevant background information and explanation for personal failures that did take place, on my part...

Back to my explanation of what took place.. The man had introduced himself with a very popular and Hebrew name from the Jewish Bible, relating to one of Judaism's beloved Biblical figures.. It wasn't actually his real name but it was a Hebrew name that he'd determined to start to go by, apparently.. He was also dressed in light colours from top to bottom, which in modern Hebrew culture may have been viewed as a type of "holy" way of dressing.

If I'd been paying careful attention and had been well-educated about common NPD (narcissistic personality disorder) traits, both of those things would have helped me to identify that the man had serious issues. "Avraham"- who on his birth certificate was named

Fidel- throughout his life had gone by the name on his birth certificate, which was very different from the Hebrew name he'd identified himself as having.

Understandably, some people, as they've gotten closer to the understanding about The LORD Jesus being a Jew from Israel, have wanted to also get closer to the Hebrew language and have a Hebrew name- so I'm not saying there's anything wrong with that at all, if it would be Elohim God's will..! That being said, I believe in this particular man's circumstance, the name he chose and the outfit he wore, were both likely chosen for tainted self-seeking purposes...

Well, as I was still sitting there, Fidel ended up deciding to tell me about a story of something he'd said had happened to him, which went maybe something like this: he'd been at a prayer meeting one night, maybe ten or more years prior, when all of a sudden it was like his body had stopped working and he may have literally physically died for a short time. It was at that time, that he'd had some type of out-of-body experience where a part of him was brought to another place. During his supposed experience, he had also apparently been shown a vision of what he later came to believe was Jerusalem, and he'd apparently also heard certain words which he believed were connecting him personally, to the Prophet Moses from The Holy Bible. Moses is one of the most famous figures in Jewish history who helped rescue the Israelites from slavery in Egypt, and was given the Ten Commandments at Mount Sinai.

I'd like to say up front that I do not- I repeat- I do not believe that all spiritual, or out-of-body experiences are from Above, whatsoever. If a person's experience- even if they were proven dead for days before returning to life- if their experience conflicts with The Word of God- then I believe that is the clear signal to be able to know for sure that their experience was not from Above, period. I believe that there is a spiritual war going on between good and evil, and that while there are "true visions," there is also a reality called "false visions."

So I don't know how much of Fidel's story was what he'd honestly experienced or not- but even he did see all of those things, etc. it still would not mean that the experience was from Above, I don't believe, nor would it mean that his interpretation was accurate. I don't know all the details of what he's said he saw, but what I know is that if it conflicted with God's Word then it was false, and the interpretation he later promoted, I do believe was a 100% false interpretation.

As I sat there, Fidel went on further about things that had happened to him in Israel in recent weeks, and with regards to the last part of his supposed experience, where he believed he had been shown he had a personal connection to the Prophet Moses.. Well the fact is that many Bible Believers still expect two more Prophets to come forth, and many may believe that one of the Prophets will have a special connection to the Prophet Moses. So, Fidel relayed about how during his recent time in Israel, he'd apparently met a number of people, etc. and whatever the details were- it ended up being that others, as well as himself, had come to believe that Fidel was literally one of the New Testament's famous two witnesses to come- and was the one with that special connection to the Prophet Moses..!!!

I believe that as Believers we do have ways we can Biblically judge Prophets and whether or not they are sent from Above or not. And I think one of those ways to help us discern is to examine the "fruit" that they bear. And so, I believe that Fidel's continuous behaviour throughout his life as a supposed Believer, has clearly helped to show that he is simply not one of the two witnesses.

Also, there are probably hundreds, if not thousands of people that have come forth even in this very generation claiming to be one of the two witnesses. So, another man proclaiming such a thing would not be something new or shocking by any means. Many may think that at that point, it should have been more than enough for me to tell the man I'd literally just met to "get lost." If I could go back, I'd love to be able to end the conversation before it even began! That being said.. unfortunately that just wasn't exactly how things transpired..

I want to please explain here that another common trait of those with NPD is that from a worldly perspective, they're often viewed as very "charming." Though he was honestly not particularly good looking by any means, either, in my opinion- there was still something about him that somehow made him such a natural leader, and he seemingly so naturally influenced people to trust him. All that being said, I personally didn't feel comfortable to just jump on board and believe that his story was true, interpretation correct, and that he was indeed one of the famous two witnesses... But at the same time, I also wasn't, at that time, prepared to reject that it may at least be a possibility.

CHAPTER 2: NARCISSISTIC TARGETING

After sharing his story with me, he asked me a very direct question, and that's when I believe some of my vulnerabilities at that time with approval-seeking, really started to rise to the surface... He pretty much asked me concerning if I believed that his interpretation was correct, and that he was truly one of the two witnesses. Due to me not feeling like I knew for sure if his interpretations were true or not, and thus me thinking there may be at least be a possibility that he was actually truly one of the famous two witnesses, I felt a deep, somewhat hidden "need" for his approval begin to come up... just in case his interpretation was correct. So when he asked me, I think I may have felt quite stuck, in that moment.

Perhaps feeling like I was in a position of weakness, having been put on the spot and feeling quite pressured... because "if he actually was one of the two witnesses," I may have thought, "I did not want to get on his bad side," so to speak... No- I wanted his approval in a very deep and possibly unconscious way- and maybe I also felt that if I didn't provide him with the answer he wanted, there was no going back and that it may negatively impact his perception of me for life, and therefore might even indicate regarding

God's stance towards me, as well!

Overly seeking approval and affirmation from other human beings can be key traits of someone with what's been labeled as *codependence*, which is a very common challenge experienced by adults who've had very difficult upbringings. Some other common traits of codependency are being very generous, giving and nurturing; and those who've struggled with codependence, happen to be the exact types of people that selfish narcissists have tended to try to prey on, and who've been susceptible to the narcissist's typical manipulative ways..! I didn't know those things at that time, though, and if someone had told me I'd had a codependency issue to address- I perhaps would not have believed them..! I was actually an incredibly independent person..! But, I've learned that there's a lot more to codependence than that alone..

So, at the time I should have obviously been able to be honest and say I didn't know at that time with certainty, one way or the other. I was also someone who was very much against lying, and who was also extremely careful with my words..! But despite how much those values meant to me, somehow being in that unusual position, where I additionally felt on the spot and pressured- I, without excuse, compromised on my morals and integrity, and in the moment allowed myself to be devalued by affirming to him that I did believe..! I believe that by making that decision, spiritually, I set myself up to be under his negative and deceptive influence, and that what I did also gave him the indication that I was someone he could control and manipulate. Thus, I believe that may have been a turning point where he determined that he was going to want to really try to target me going forward.

This is also where a very real seed of what, I believe, can be termed as spiritual abuse was planted. I think there may be a number of great definitions or explanations out there concerning what spiritual abuse is- but with regards to this story- I'd perhaps describe it, at least in part, as: someone using their perceived spiritual authority or position to effectively control or manipulate others..; an abuse that may often also involve sexual immorality. The negative effects of that seed may not have been completely obvious at first, but within a short period of time, many things did become much more apparent..!

Another highly important detail regarding the first time I met Fidel, is that I believe it may have been more towards the end of that first interaction, when he casually did say that he was married.. Of course, I'm not sure I ever saw him wearing a wedding ring during the entire period of having been in communication with him.. And despite any excuse that he may have had with regards to his failure to wear his wedding ring- of jewelry making him uncomfortable, or whatever, and his wife being well aware of his issues with jewelry... in his particular case- again, I do believe that those were even further loud warning signals that helped to show that he was a narc and was not to be trusted..! Why did a married man feel the need to stop and talk to me- about a supposed spiritual experience he'd had the first place? Sharing about The LORD Jesus Christ may have been one thing, but why would he have taken it so much further?

But he did such a good job, I thought, of not coming across as interested in me in "that way"- and I was just so naive to think that he may be speaking to me in 100% purity. His stance towards me, however, did prove not to be what I'd have hoped, by any means. And his actions alone in that one meeting, as a married man, should have been more than enough for me to want nothing to do with him. I'm truly embarrassed that I just still had so much to learn at that time.. But the fact is that many women have gone through similar things with older, cunning, married men.. I was not the first, and I was not the last. And especially with the background I'd had, coupled with the lack of knowledge concerning certain weaknesses that I needed to work though that I wasn't even aware I'd had, I was simply in a vulnerable position, and that's a fact...

I believe the adversary knew the exact type of scenario that would be most likely to "get me" even if nothing else would... As the Bible-believer that I am, with the things I still needed to work out, what person's approval would I want more than someone who I thought may actually be a modern-day Biblical character..?!?! In fact, prior to even meeting Fidel, I believe I'd literally thought about, how if I was ever able to meet one of the two witnesses- something maybe along the lines of: that I would want him to confirm to me that I had God's approval..! So I had a serious lesson to learn after all of this concerning not putting anyone on any type of pedestal in such a manner, etc... but that's another story...

Something else I would like to please note, and another major lesson that I learned, is that despite Fidel eventually stating that he was married, I mistakenly may have actually allowed that to be used as something to influence me to trust him *more* rather than *less.* "Since, obviously if he was truly a follower of God, and especially a famous Last Days Prophet- he'd never have any impure intentions towards any female other than his wife, right?!" Hmm..! Not to mention, he specifically shared that it wasn't typical for him to be going around and stopping to talk to random females, sort of thing... Later on, however, I believe that he did in fact prove to be quite the fast-moving "ladies man" indeed- but more on that, a bit later..!

Making Plans

So I didn't know about all of that at the time, and while he and his friend had actually been in a rush to meet someone at the airport, Fidel had held them up in order to stop all that they were doing, and approach me- a total stranger. I think he may have even tried to portray to me that there, thus, must have been something very spiritual and special about the entire encounter..! How he'd literally stopped all they were doing and felt some type of pull to come and speak to me..!?!?

Well actually that was just another typical narc tactic- trying to make the subject feel as if there is an extraordinary "once in a lifetime" connection between them.. Also it can play a role in the 1st part of the typical narc cycle, where the narc acts very loving and attentive, as they try to gain the subject's trust and make the subject become attached to and dependant on the narc.. I have, thankfully, learned a ton since that time- however, at that time I don't even recall having ever heard of the term NPD in my life, and there was still going to be a lot for me to learn…

Once Fidel had succeeded in influencing me to confirm to him that I believed that he was one of the two witnesses, I believe it was on- and to him I was high prey. I still hoped and thought he had pure intentions towards me, and I didn't recognize, or recognize enough, what a big deal it was- what had just happened. But I believe those were important lessons I'd be learning concerning, going forward.

Though I didn't have much of a social life during those 4 years, I did still have some social interaction, particularly around "feast" seasons when many may be visiting from out of town, etc. And, I believe, it just so happened to be one of those seasons! I'd actually been supposed to meet some other Believers I knew later that day- one of them actually also being Spanish-speaking himself- so it seemed "perfect" for us all to meet and for me to invite Fidel and his friend along… We exchanged contact information and planned to meet again later that day when the other Believers were present… and that's what we all did. We had all met in the Old City of Jerusalem, and walked to the downtown area of Jerusalem together. I think that on the walk, Fidel even actually told one of my friends about his "vision story," as well.

And it wasn't like I was the only one who'd considered that Fidel being one of the two witnesses may be a possibility..! Nor was it like he'd needed to seclude people to follow him so he could indoctrinate them for months and form a cult, or anything..! I guess I really perhaps just can't explain how or why people would literally meet the man over a short period of time and somehow seemingly be convinced that he may be one of the two witnesses- but that is literally what seemed to happen over and over again..!!! Even our Bible study leaders who were well known in the community, while initially seeming guarded- did seem to eventually "come around" and actually also really want to be on his good side!!!

Now that I reflect concerning it, I can think of three specific things that Fidel may have tried to use to help him influence and manipulate people to go along with him. First of all, from the world's standpoint, I believe Fidel was very "charming"- which is a classic trait of a narcissist. He also allegedly had a history of working at a very large Christian TV channel, where he was apparently exposed to the rich and famous- and apparently saw "from the inside" some of the things that were going on that may have been "corrupt," so to speak. That in itself, made him unique and may have been something he tried to use to give him that much more perceived authority, credibility, and status. It may have helped "build his case" as someone who was there to try to expose darkness, and so on... "Who else was in a position to expose such things, than someone who'd had such direct interactions, right?!" Hmm...

On top of all of that, he seemed to be pretty well-off financially- though I believe it was his wife who was the one that was working full-time throughout his travels, and that it was she, herself, who came from a wealthy family... As far as his personal financial contribution to their household, that I perhaps cannot comment on one way or the other, and is information I may truly not have been privy to... but as far as his interactions in Israel- I can comment that I think it was not irregular for him to be spending money on those around him, and so on... Money has very typically be used by narcissists to try to control their subjects. There are different ways they have used money for control, whether being the financial provider or not- but regardless of which method pursued- classically, money is a major narcissistic tool.

Anyways, as it was getting a bit later and people were going to be leaving shortly. I believe it was around that time, that Fidel actually invited me on a future group weekend road trip that would be taking place with people he knew. Thinking he might be one of the two witnesses, I was definitely glad to stay in contact with him, and as I'd mentioned- at that time, I also had a huge empty space in my life with regards to community... So I had that vulnerability and was perhaps enduring quite a bit of isolation, as well as quite a bit of stress, with regards to the particular living situation I'd found myself in at that time... Additionally, and unbeknownst to me, as far as the codependence that I had and was needing to overcome, one of the traits could involve trusting too easily... So for Fidel, being a narcissist, to meet me- a single woman who had all of those factors combined, at that time... in that type of scenario, really did make me a prime target..! We had our plans, said our goodbyes, and that was that.

Fidel's Sister

The first day of the scheduled group-trip arrived, and Fidel's sister Sierra would actually be flying into Israel and joining along. She was going to be landing in Israel that day, so the plan was that the three of us would spend some time together in Jerusalem's Old City, before meeting one of Fidel's friends Andreas, and then all 4 of us would be traveling together from Jerusalem to Andreas' house in Northern Israel where we'd be staying for the weekend with his family.

Once I'd met Sierra, the three of us went to a number of places, showing her around Jerusalem... Eventually we stopped for lunch at a local Israeli restaurant, and after we'd been sitting there for a little while- unexpectedly the two of them had ended up getting into some type of disagreement..! I tried to help diffuse the situation and they did end up working things out, so that at least for the time being, they would be continuing on with the trip together...

Somehow, though, despite the brief tension that had taken place between them, *even his sister* seemed to also be going along with the idea of him being one of the two witnesses- at least to a certain extent..! And later on that day, when the three of us had gone to a nearby Christian museum, even the man who worked there seemed to be thinking it was a serious possibility! Yes, Fidel was talking about his "vision story" and being one of the two witnesses, over and over again- even to people he'd just met! And somehow, people seemed to be drawn in time and again..!

CHAPTER 3: NARCISSISM UNMASKED- WHAT EXACTLY IS NPD?

Narcissistic Personality Disorder (NPD) is a serious personality disorder that has been studied about in the field of psychology. Narcissists (who may also be referred to as narcs) tend to be highly manipulative and controlling, and there are a number of types of narcissists, with some being much more cruel and vindictive than others... While narcissists may know how to act very loving and attentive, they have one "true love," and that is themselves. It may not always be obvious, but narcissists want to be admired and have an inappropriate sense of self-entitlement. They lack appropriate empathy for others, and rather exploit certain people around them... Narcissists can be arrogant, rude, and envious- but believe they are the ones who are envied. They also, however, can be great actors and may come across as very likeable, sensitive and considerate to others..!

There is a 3-part cycle that narcissists typically go through, during which, at least some of their true character does get exposed.. That cycle is written about in further detail, along with more important information about NPD, in Chapter 9 of this book.

Please note: The word "psychology" is related to the Greek word "psyche" that is actually connected with the word "soul." I don't agree with, nor would I promote, all of what's been taught within the so-called field of psychology- but I do think when sifting carefully- there is valuable information to uncover..

Npd Warning Signs

We've already pointed out a lot of narcissistic warning signs that took place up until this point in the narrative, which I'd now like to look into a bit further... We'll have a 2nd very telling review, as we continue forward- but regarding the information that we've covered so far, I believe there is already an incredible amount of valuable data to learn..!

1. Fidel often wearing light clothing, from top to bottom.

In that type of religiously-minded environment, so to speak, that light coloured clothing that Fidel wore from top to bottom was likely a tool to try to help project an image of "holiness," and try to influence others to trust and regard him as someone with authority. Of course, however, anyone can wear light clothing, so to speak, so what may be far more important to consider about a person, rather than what color clothing they wear- is the type of spiritual fruit they put forth.

> *Beware of false prophets, which come to you in sheep's clothing, but inwardly they are ravening wolves. Ye shall know them by their fruits. Do men gather grapes of thorns, or figs of thistles? Even so every good tree bringeth forth good fruit; but a corrupt tree bringeth forth evil fruit. A good tree cannot bring forth evil fruit, neither can a corrupt tree bring forth good fruit. Every tree that bringeth not forth good fruit is hewn down, and cast into the fire. Wherefore by their fruits ye shall know them.*
>
> *Matthew 7:15-20 *edAKJV, The Holy Bible*
>
> *For such are false apostles, deceitful workers, transforming*

themselves into the apostles of Christ. And no marvel; for satan himself is transformed into an angel of light. Therefore it is no great thing if his ministers also be transformed as the ministers of righteousness; whose end shall be according to their works.

*2 Corinthians 11:13-15 *edAKJV, The Holy Bible*

2. Fidel's victim/hero stories.

Narcissists are known to be highly manipulative, and Fidel was no exception. One example is about how Fidel had relayed a story to me when I'd been sitting on that platform that first time we'd met, that maybe went something like this: at some point during his recent visit to Israel, he'd been spending time with some of his new friends, which apparently included several men, who all considered him being one of the two witnesses…! He even relayed about a supposed event that had taken place, where he'd left his friends to be alone in a room and was perhaps considering "running away from his calling," so to speak, and leaving Israel… One of his friends apparently went to speak to him, and somehow with regards to their interaction, I believe, he was connecting his experience and the desire to leave Israel, to The Book of Jonah in The Holy Bible, of when the Prophet Jonah had resisted doing what he had been meant to do…!

I believe his story was highly manipulative, and a way to try to add that much more perceived weight behind the idea of him really being one of the two witnesses. Him, first of all, supposedly having others who gave credit to the idea, was something I believe he tried to use as a manipulative tactic to try to influence me to also think it was a possibility, etc. I also believe Fidel's story may have been a way of not only trying to play the victim, but to also try to portray himself as a type of hero- all at the same time..! I believe he may have depicted that he'd chosen to make a sacrifice and stay in Israel to do what he was "supposed" to do, despite being "tempted to leave." Portraying oneself as either the victim or the hero is a classic narcissistic tactic. Narcissists may often share stories from their past where they are depicted as one or the other. In the above example (though there may be others..), it seems Fidel might have actually found a way to be depicted as both the victim and the hero in one single story!

3. Fidel pressuring me to state what I believed about him being one of the two witnesses, and putting me on the spot...

I believe this may have been a way of testing me to see if he could control, manipulate and spiritually abuse me.. Narcissists want people around them that they can control, manipulate and deceive.

4. Fidel sharing about his "vision story" and belief that he was one of the two witnesses, repeatedly- even with complete strangers.

Narcissists love to talk about... *themselves*- and they love the conversation and focus to be on them! One of the most important things to them is their perceived status, and to them- the more highly people think of them, the better.

5. Fidel speaking about how he'd felt to stop and talk to me of all people, even when he and his friend had been in a rush to be somewhere- and how it was something he typically did not do...

Trying to make me feel like there was something particularly "special" about "our connection," was a classic narcissistic tool. Narcissists classically try to convince their subjects that there is something unique and special about their connection with their target, and that it's even "once in a lifetime."

6. Things going very quickly.

Fidel and I had just met, but all of a sudden he'd invited me to meet with him and his sister alone, and from there to be going on an actual road trip with them, and stay at his friend's house- someone whom I'd never even met before..!? Going really quickly from the beginning, can be another classic narcissistic trait; and unfortunately, going really quickly can also be a classic codependency weakness- so those who have struggled with codependence have perhaps needed to be all the more guarded concerning it..!

7. Fidel's identity.

Narcissists typically try to make themselves into the image of what they believe their subjects want them to be. From the clothes that he wore, to the name that he went by, it seems Fidel may have been changing his supposed taste, and even a layer of his identity, like a chameleon in order to match the atmosphere around him and increase his likelihood of being liked and trusted... Narcissists are known to change their supposed preferences to match their subjects, and that can include their style of clothing, musical taste, stated interests, etc. It seems that Fidel was trying to influence the people around him to view him as a holy Prophet, and that that was the type of image he wanted to project.

An important note about narcissistic warning signs: in order to be a narcissist, a person doesn't have to display all of the possible narcissist warning signs, and likewise in order not to be a narcissist, a person doesn't have to lack all of the possible narcissist warning signs. Also, the above list is not an exhaustive list of possible narcissistic warning signs, what so ever, but it is a list of preliminary narcissistic warning signs that may have taken place within just that short amount of time. Signs, that if I'd been able to identify, I might have made much better choices with regards to- and ended all communication with Fidel right from the beginning... If I'd really been highly aware and discerning about NPD at that time, then I'd have recognized within the first moments of meeting him or so, the type of person that he was..!

CHAPTER 4:
ISOLATION-
ENEMY TACTIC

The time arrived for Fidel, his sister Sierra, and I, to meet Fidel's friend Andreas who would be bringing us to his house in Northern Israel for our weekend-long road trip. Andreas joined the three of us in Jerusalem and then all four of us walked together to the designated local bus stop. After the first shorter bus ride, we all caught a second bus which was going to be quite a bit longer than the first- maybe around two and a half hours... For that bus ride, I was seated next to Fidel's sister Sierra with whom I'd gotten along quite well, until that point, and who's company I had enjoyed quite a bit... In fact, being a bit older than me, I'd perhaps even "looked up to her" in a sense.

Eventually we did all arrive at the Andreas' house, and it was arranged that Fidel, Sierra, and I would be doing a separate "mini-trip" that day. The time came for us to go on our outing, after which, we'd planned to return to Andreas' house and have a "Shabbat dinner" with himself and the rest of his small family. To briefly explain, "Shabbat dinner" is a dinner that is held by many Jews (as well as some Bible-believing non-Jews) every Friday, around or after sunset… "'Shabbat" is the word in Hebrew, but in English it's called "Sabbath." It's viewed as a weekly rest day, where work is not to be done for around 24 hours, and ends around or after sunset on Saturday. It is also viewed as a holy day..! There's a lot more information about the Sabbath in The Bible, of course, as well, including The New Testament.

The time to go on the "mini-trip" arrived, and the three of us were off… This time, though, we traveled by taxi… Once again, it was not so long into the outing and a conflict between Fidel and Sierra had erupted once more.. Unlike last time, however, things began to seriously crumble between the two of them and I found myself caught in the middle..! After having visited one popular site, the three of us had actually made it to a body of water where Sierra had been supposed to be baptized by Fidel. Apparently this may have been supposed to be the highlight of her entire trip to Israel and the main reason she'd traveled there in the first place..! And yet there they were in an almost "seemingly out of nowhere" huge argument and she was threatening to leave…

I think Fidel may have already been in the water, when she began to speak to me negatively about her brother… I'd actually thought that just prior to that, she had been open regarding him being one of the two witnesses- so the anger she seemed to have towards him may have really caught me off guard, so to speak.. She actually started to speak about the past and I believe it was actually at that time, that she told me that all of their other siblings had an issue with him and she'd even been warned by one of her siblings not go to to Israel, because of him! On top of that, she told me that Fidel had been married a total of… 8 times..!

Not to sound judgemental, and not that everyone who has been married that many times has for sure struggled with NPD, but that was most definitely another huge warning sign! As culturally acceptable as divorce has been in recent history- being married 8 times may still be very extreme by literally anyone's standards..! Even, just about unheard of..!

Well, Fidel didn't hear all that she was saying to me, I don't believe- and finally he seemed to want to continue forward with the plans we'd had- which included me getting re-baptized, as well... As far as his sister, though, I think he may have seemed agreeable to just letting her leave, if that was what she wanted to do. And that's exactly what she did do... but not before- again, seemingly out of nowhere- accusing him of, maybe something along the lines of- using her as a way of trying to get closer to *me* and still come across as innocent! It seems to me that it was during that "mini-trip" that she had begun to really get clarity about Fidel's manipulative NPD ways, and recognize that she should not have trusted him to be acting in innocence with regards to me.

But the fact is that while she may have been well acquainted with his history- I was not. He was the one that had introduced me to her, and I was still thinking he may be one of the two witnesses. So while I had gotten along with her well until that point, I don't believe that overpowered my perceived relationship with him. I was being very ignorant concerning keeping strong boundaries with him, as the married man that he was, and as far as her accusations of him- I was not necessarily in a place where I was ready to believe everything she was saying. So despite, perhaps, thinking and expressing that we should maybe leave with her, or try to do something to stop her from going- she did leave and Fidel allowed it, and I chose to stay there with him, rather than leave with her.

While I see things very differently now, I pretty much thought that the accusation she'd made about him wanting to get closer to me, had zero validity- and to that point I simply hadn't consciously sensed him having any type of romantic interest in me... While the accusation she'd made about him being married 8 times did surprise me- I don't know that I was prepared to try to make any "final judgements" concerning it without asking him about it first, etc.; but even that wasn't something I was necessarily so eager to confront him about, since I was still perhaps quite stuck in wanting his "approval" and thinking he might be one of the two witnesses..!

So, even though we seemed to be in an extremely remote location-Sierra actually did end up leaving..! And that left me and Fidel in a private location with no one else around for the first time, I believe, ever..! That was just one more thing that simply should not have happened, and something that, even at that time, I do think I may have typically very much avoided... But, as I'd said, he'd gotten into the water to baptized his sister who clearly opted out, and next he was going to baptize me. Perhaps somewhat reluctantly, feeling pulled in two different directions between Fidel and his sister- I did go ahead and also get into the water, and allow him to "baptize" me as well. Fidel and I did leave that location not so long later, and managed to find our way back to Andreas' house... It was when we arrived there, though, that things started to get extremely uncomfortable for me.

Change Of Plans

It was within maybe just seconds of arriving at Andreas' house, that Sierra had said something that seemed to show that she wasn't only upset with Fidel, but clearly had animosity against me, as well..! That compounded things for me drastically because, I had already been uncomfortable with the host Andreas who had made a comment while we had all still been in Jerusalem that I'd felt was disrespectful towards me. So while his comment had had nothing directly to do with Fidel what so ever- to arrive back at his house after the "mini-trip, gone wrong" and find that there was an additional issue, but this time between me and Sierra... I can't say that was something I was happy about, to say the least..!

So despite all of those things, I think at that point I was still trying to keep pressing forward and be positive.. it wasn't like there seemed to be many further options..?! Shabbat was approaching-the rest day where busses would not be running and most stores would be closed.. and it was a day I had personally been quite dedicated to wanting to keep for years..! It wasn't long at all before the evening drew in and we were all sitting down for dinner together;

at which time, to my horror- even the host's wife Sofia began to insistently treat me in a way that, to me, was also very upsetting..! While what she was doing, also did not directly having to do with Fidel, at all- it still symbolized to me a major shift of the entire trip's experience. Tragically, it was with regards to her persistent treatment towards me at that dinner table, that I perceived myself as being clearly isolated from every single adult in that entire house- other than Fidel himself..!

While from a narcissist's standpoint, that would have been an absolutely amazing scenario to have one's subject in- for me, that was obviously not a good scenario, at all..! There I was, in an unfamiliar city, at night, and during the Sabbath..! I was feeling isolated from all of the other adults in that house, and yet still viewed Fidel- the narcissist- as a possibly true and highly favoured, Biblically famous Prophet of God!? From a narcissist's standpoint, a scenario like that might as well have been scripted..!

After dinner, despite very much not wanting to even be in that house, and despite the extreme discomfort that I had begun to feel, which would perhaps simply be impossible to describe with words- we all sat in the living room together... The host, Andreas, played guitar and sang... And eventually, I ended up also singing and playing some of my own songs on guitar, as well... Fidel was intently listening to me as I played, which is another classic narcissistic trait- with regards to the first phase of The 3-Phase Classic Narcissistic Cycle (as described in more detail in Chapter 9). It wasn't that late at night, but the rest of the group had eventually left the living room, and were actually settling down for bed.. I wasn't in any rush to go to bed, being so uncomfortable with the rest of the group, so I was quite content (and ignorant) to be willing to continue on alone with Fidel in the living room..!

And it wasn't long before conflict erupted, again..! It seemed that the host Andreas and his wife were not comfortable with me and Fidel being alone together in the living room at night.. As much as I may take very strong issue with several things that they did during that short time I was acquainted with them, having an issue with me and Fidel being alone together, despite me seemingly not really having anywhere to turn- I do support..! Well, they said whatever they said, and though I may have been nowhere near to feeling like I was ready to go to sleep- I determined to just go along with their preference, and go back to the bedroom I had been designated to sleep in… I was miserable in that house, extremely uncomfortable, and literally couldn't stand it there, but what could I do..?!

It may have all seemed to somewhat come out of nowhere, but I'd only been in that bedroom for a very short time, and Fidel ended up announcing that he was actually leaving..! He maybe said something like "anyone who wants to come, can come- but regardless, I am leaving!" Narcissists do not like to be exposed, so the fact that the other adults were taking issue with him, so to speak, might have just been too much for him handle..! At that point, I was not in a good place with any of them, and still didn't recognize that there was a huge issue with Fidel to watch out for… So, as isolated as I already was, he may have clearly seen an opportunity to try to take advantage of the circumstances, and isolate me even further.. and maybe not surprisingly, I responded that I would go with him!

What a disaster! As much as being in that house with those people may have seemed like a type of frightening and miserable torture, and I may have had every reason not to want to be around them, what so ever- being off alone with a married man at night, I'd have hopefully clearly known, was also not an ideal circumstance by any means; 2 witnesses or not..! To take things a step further- it was the Sabbath, and we were in an unfamiliar city. Being the Sabbath, while some businesses did remain open, many of them were shut down. The busses would not be running until much later the next day, and I was not someone who spent money on the Sabbath, anyways..!

CHAPTER 5: THE MOMENT OF TRUTH

Fidel and I left Andreas' house that night by foot, with our things on our arms- a particularly "non-Shabbat suitable" thing to do- to be carrying heavy materials... He was pretty much leading the way, as we walked, and walked, and walked. I still thought he may be one of the two witnesses, and had not felt, to that point, like he had romantic interest in me... So as much as, under normal circumstances, I may have not chosen to be alone with him at night- I did accept that we seemed to be stuck in that situation. With my guard down, my boundaries needing to be adjusted, and unaddressed codependency issues- at least a part of me did, regretfully, appreciate the perceived opportunity for us to be able to get to know each other on a deeper level which I still had the misguided expectation of, as being pure.

Finally, we did get to a beachfront that had a small hotel nearby. We ended up staying there on the beach, and continuing to speak for a long while.. He told me about things that he'd supposedly been through in his past, which I believe included a supposed "secret" that I was supposed to keep concerning his past experiences... Him supposedly trusting me with a secret would have been a great manipulative tactic to try to continue to make me feel "special"- as if he was trusting me with sensitive information, and continue to strengthen my sense of loyalty towards him...

Despite it being late at night, it wasn't particularly cold outside, and I think that I personally would have been fine with just trying to find a place to lie down outside, and waiting for the day to arrive.. Fidel, on the other hand, it may have seemed, wanted to try to find an actual hotel to stay at..! I think the idea of staying at a hotel was concerning to me, as it was the Sabbath, and I didn't believe in conducting financial transactions or causing anyone to work on that day..

I think I may have clarified to him that if we did go to a hotel, it would be 2 separate rooms, and that they'd have to agree for the payment to be made the next day after sunset (once the Sabbath was over).. Even with those stipulations in place, I think I still may have been pretty uneasy with the whole idea of staying at a hotel.. Whether paid after the Sabbath or not, I also didn't want people to have to work because of me on The Sabbath- such as, arranging which room would be designated for me, and so on. Yet, that being said, I was still looking up to Fidel as a possible highly authoritative spiritual leader, so there were sadly only so many waves I was going to make, at that time.

He went to speak to the hotel personnel while I stayed at the beachfront, waiting for him to return. He did return not so long later, seemingly excited about how he'd sorted something great out for us..! He'd apparently negotiated an amazing price with them, due to it already being so late at night, etc. And while, it just so happened they only had one final room available- it seemed the way he may have wanted me to see it, was that I should still be so thankful that they had any space at all..! In retrospect, it is clear that the hotel may have had more rooms available after all, but either way, that was the supposed circumstance at the time..! Fidel assured me that he would sleep on the floor, and I regret to report, that while I may have had some hesitation, I did go along with the arrangement...

He returned to the hotel, but this time I went with him, and we took the room that he'd told me about so enthusiastically. He took a space on the floor, as he'd said he would, and I took the bed. The night was going to finally end but it would only be within a matter of hours that I was going to finally start to *get* that something was terribly wrong. What happened, maybe went something like this: we were in the room relaxing, and he showed me a ring that he'd purchased as a gift for his wife.. It was brand new and had Scripture written on it, from what may be commonly viewed as the most romantic book in the entire Bible, Song of Songs. That was when- he suggested for me to try it on...

To me, that just did not seem right, and so I declined his suggestion. I think he may have persisted, but I held my ground. I did not try on that ring and I wasn't going to try it on. It just didn't seem right to me- and with good reason..! It was a romantic gift for his wife, after all..! How would she feel to receive a supposedly special and romantic gift from him, knowing that he'd had some other woman put it on her own finger..?! No, I wasn't going to do that... And it was after that happened, that I finally started to feel a sense that maybe Fidel actually did have romantic feelings towards me. I think I may have still needed time to process things, and it was going to be about time to start getting on with the day...

I went to take a shower and while I was in the bathroom I heard some type of noise outside the bathroom and thought Fidel may have even messed around with the bathroom door. I think at that point, I went to be sure the door was locked, and that was when things finally did begin to hit me... I think it was at that point that I was really starting to see that something truly was off, after all, and I think I may have felt a sense of distress come over me, as I think I may have begun to consider how I might actually try to get away from him...

Exposed

Despite finally having clarity that something was off in Fidel's stance towards me, I still somehow was stuck under the delusion of thinking that he may still be one of the greatest spiritual leaders of this generation, and potentially one of God's most favoured people in history..! So, as I think I was still working through some of my own personal insecurities concerning God's love and approval towards me, I think I may have still very much wanted to keep Fidel's approval, as a way of supposedly helping to confirm God's stance towards me.

It was the next day and Fidel had arranged for the hotel to give us access to a pass that would allow us into nearby private beachfront. Again these were things I'd have preferred not to even be indirectly involved with on the Sabbath in that manner- arranging things with hotel workers, etc.- but I was sadly just not standing with 100% strength at that time, what so ever, with regards to standing for what I believed in... It was before we left the hotel to go to that beachfront, when I seemed to feel God may be showing me that it was going to be time for me to take off. And so the moment of truth was quickly approaching, so to speak. I had to make a decision and I had to make it fast... Would I do what I thought God may be showing me to do, and flee Fidel's presence... or would I continue to spend the day with Fidel and eventually return to Jerusalem with him once the Sabbath was over..?

I may have realized that if I did take off and flee, that that may permanently damage my relationship with Fidel, and that he may never think as "highly" of me, as he supposedly did, ever again... But whether Fidel was a true Prophet or not- I should have trusted my own perception of what I thought God may want me to do, rather than letting someone I barely even knew lead me.

True- I was in a somewhat unfamiliar city, in a somewhat unfamiliar region of the country; many places may be closed, and I'd pretty much be "stuck" in that region until Shabbat was over... But I don't think those "challenges" were really of great concern to me at all, nor that they'd have needed to be. Trying to find a public beach or safe spot to sit until until after sunset, when I'd be able to take a bus home- I don't think was really such an intimidating or overwhelming idea to me at all.. I was very "well-traveled," very independent, and had tons of life experience. Even if I wasn't so familiar with that particular region, I was in a country that I was highly connected to as a Jew, and it was also a more "peaceful time" in Israel's recent history..

So truthfully- I don't believe those were my issues with leaving, what so ever... I believe my issue with leaving was risking losing the "approval" of someone I still thought might be one of the two witnesses. It's like I was literally under a certain level of brain- wash! It seems to me that from that first time I'd met him, by letting myself feel pressured to go ahead and confirm to him that I thought he was one of the two witnesses- that it may have liter- ally influenced me to actually believe it- or to at least consider it to be such a strong possibility- despite having not first diligently "tested his fruit"!

So there I was, facing the truth verses Fidel's facade. I wanted that man's "approval" so strongly to the point that I may have even thought it would help confirm God's approval of me, yet at the same time, I thought that God might be showing me to leave..! Feeling something may be off... Feeling like he may have feelings towards me that were not appropriate...!!! So now it came down to deciding what I was going to let influence my decision and who I was going to trust. Would I trust *myself* and my sense that I might have been shown from Above that it was time to take off and flee from the situation?! Or would I trust a supposed "spiritual leader" and "authority" to direct me, and let him lead me to a beach...??? And so, it seems that I, unfortunately, was just so out for Fidel's ap- proval and was perhaps not feeling 100% certain regarding what God wanted me to do- without having more time to contemplate between the two choices- very regrettably went to the beachfront.

We had not been at the private beach for very long when Fidel seemed to sense that something was different, and mentioned something about it to me... I responded by pretty openly- telling him about how I felt, and I think I might have not only specifically mentioned my concerns about the ring and the door, but even that I thought he may have feelings for me..! I think I also may have also tried to console myself that I could have a better conscience after having been up front with him concerning those things... But not surprisingly, he remained very casual about the things I'd said and seemingly still wanted to keep going forward as if nothing was wrong..! So while I was perhaps trying to comfort myself that in speaking up- I'd supposedly "stood my ground" and "brought things to light," and "everything was fine"- the truth was that even though I may have had the courage to share from my concerns, what I did was obviously just not enough..!!! And so the plain and simple truth is, that I should have left. Once I knew something seemed off, and I'd even thought I might have been shown from Above that it was time to leave- there's perhaps just no other way to put it: I should have left.

CHAPTER 6: THE WRONG PATH

During our short time at that beachfront, Fidel had been trying to pressure me to be baptized yet again..! I believe he portrayed that he felt "from Above" that I needed to do it again, even though I'd just been "baptized" the other day with him...!?!?! I had opposition to it, however- perhaps simply not wanting to be close to him physically or to allow him to touch me with regards to it. He did pressure me though, and eventually I did cave and got in the water and let him "baptize" me once more...!!!!!! Classically, narcissists are controlling and want to control their subjects.

We finally left the beach, and eventually evening came... We had our things packed up, left the hotel, and went to the bus stop... The bus arrived and before long we were on it and heading back to Jerusalem. On the bus, I did start to notice something seemed off, inside of me... As the bus was perhaps getting more and more crowded- Fidel and I were in seats next to one another, and there'd been a woman on the bus, to whom Fidel had almost offered his seat... Since the bus may have been starting to fill up- it was truly a great narcissistic opportunity to try to "innocently" triangulate me, in an attempt to try to make me jealous or tempted to try to fight for him- while of course still maintaining an image of selflessness, righteousness, and innocence, etc. I was already in a place where I was clearly letting him "walk all over me," so to speak, by allowing him to continually control me, etc. so he may have figured such a tactic may work perfectly against me, at that time... Unfortunately, the results may have been exactly what he'd wanted, because, it may have been right after that happened that I did start to sense inside of me that the stance I had towards him was simply "off" in some way..!

Finally the bus arrived back in Jerusalem, and from there Fidel wanted to get something to eat... I stayed around as he ordered from a fast food restaurant, and finally the night was over and I left on my own to go home. That wasn't before we'd made plans, however, for me to return his things to him the next day, as he and his sister had left some of their things at my apartment before we'd left for the trip. The fact that he had things at my place is also a classic narc tactic of *entangling*... they entangle their lives with their subjects' lives in an attempt to make it that much harder for the subject to get away from them!

My last bus ride home on my own was not particularly eventful, other than the fact that towards the end of the journey, several things happened around me that somehow really started to give me the feeling that God may be actually warning me about Fidel... Then, that same night- after I went to sleep- I had a powerful dream concerning him that I believe was very much from Above..! In that dream, I believe I was shown maybe something like: that I'd wronged Fidel's wife and she was rightfully very upset with me and justifiably wanted nothing to do with me..! I think I may have also been shown that somehow, someway, I'd begun to develop feelings for Fidel that were not appropriate..! I do believe that dream was very much from Above, and that by not fleeing when I believed I may have been shown to do so- somehow it put me in a position where I'd become vulnerable to developing inappropriate feelings towards him...!!! It was very clear to me that I needed to cut all contact with him, and whether he was one of the two witnesses or not was 100% irrelevant..!!!

I think after waking from that dream I may have been pretty surprised, because while I had noticed myself feel something during the bus ride back- which I'd perhaps tried to push away and ignore - I am not sure I had even fully realized I'd developed feelings for him..! None the less, I accepted the dream's message, which I do believe to have been 100% true- and recognized that I had in fact developed inappropriate feelings towards Fidel... Despite the position I found myself in- I think I may have also felt very thankful to have clarity concerning things, and that I knew what to do. I simply needed to end communication with him, and that was that.

So that next day, as I had agreed with Fidel I would do, I went to return his things to him... While I was there, I told him that I needed to "cut ties," or whatever. Unfortunately for me, though, he did put up a major fight and did not seem even close to ready to simply accept what I had to say about it..! I tried to patiently explain to him that I'd had a dream and felt clearly that was what I needed to do, etc... I believe he may have kept trying to press me about the topic of whether or not I was shown I had feelings for him, with relation to why I needed to break away from him... and I think I may have simply tried to avoid getting specifically into that question- and rather, continued to try to reason with him, so that he would let me walk away in peace, so to speak, rather than feel like I was slamming a door in his face...

It turned into what was maybe over an hour of me trying to patiently help explain to him that I'd felt I'd been shown things in a dream, and that I could not continue to spend time with him, etc... He obviously was not accepting that easily, whatsoever, and was rather actually trying to convince me to go out with him to eat!!! Finally after quite a lot of time had passed, I even finally felt myself briefly acting frustrated towards him- something I especially did not want to do towards who I thought might be "one of the two witnesses"- but I seemed to be getting to my limit..! Well, despite him wanting for us to "go out to eat"- I stood my ground, and finally walked away.

To briefly address regarding how I still could have thought Fidel might be one of the two witnesses... despite what had happened, and despite the clarity I seemed to have found- as far as cutting ties with him- I do believe I was still not fully free, by any means, of what I believe to have been a deception, as far as that's concerned. I believe I was also, very much, too lenient in my judgement and may have wrongfully justified and reasoned that "even if he had crossed a line with me with the ring," and "even if he'd had inappropriate feelings towards me"- that "even a Last Days prophet might have certain weaknesses"...

While I do, of course, think a Last Days prophet is human, and there are many "great" Biblical characters who have made huge mistakes.. I do think those two scenarios are entirely different. For instance: King David, one of my absolute favorite historical Biblical figures. A highly beloved and well-respected Biblical and royal ancestor, who did unarguably commit adultery, impregnate the man's wife, and then deceptively try to have him killed- seemingly to help prevent being "caught." Sounds pretty serious, right? And it was! But here is what I believe to be the huge difference between what King David did verses Fidel's actions. What King David did, I believe, was on impulse- and when confronted with it by The Prophet Samuel, he was fully and extremely repentant. I believe that Fidel's actions, on the other hand, were calculated; and that type of behavior was simply a part of his everyday character.

There's a huge difference between someone wanting to walk the right path, regretfully mis-stepping here and there along the way, but always repenting and being grieved by their mistakes- verses sin being a part of someone's actual character and everyday lifestyle, without any true change or personal conviction concerning their wrongs... So while God is The Judge- I not only absolutely do not think Fidel is one of the two witnesses, but actually think that unless he would truly repent of and confess regarding the type of behaviour he was engaged in (while not only proclaiming to be part of The Body of Christ- but representing that he may even be one of the highest leaders within The entire Body!!!) there may be huge risk with regards to his actual salvation..!!!

So to this point it might seem like things would be headed in a good direction for me personally... Despite my weaknesses, God has provided me with a way out in His grace and mercies, right? Well, I do believe that is it 100% true that God did provide me with a way out in His grace and mercies. But unfortunately, things did not end up going the way they truly should have... While I did leave that day, and I did refuse his idea of us going out to eat- unfortunately, it turned out that I was not willing to hold onto my strong resolve and stand by the decision to cut contact with him. I was at a place in my life where I was not only somewhat isolated and struggling with the unaddressed codependence, but I was also just finishing getting through the final stages of a difficult, stressful, and very negative roommate situation... I was perhaps feeling very hurt, mistreated, and betrayed- and due to not being able to yet enter into a long-term contact, I was also struggling with regards to having a sense of stability. So I found myself, once more, looking to move to yet another new place of residence, etc. and with all the challenges I was facing at that time, while "alone" overseas- being actively pursued by a man that I still thought may be one of the "two witnesses" was so regrettably not something I was going to have the determination to shut down.

Given all that had happened with Fidel, and especially as someone who had a true relationship with God and wanted to be a "good person"- it should have been clear and it should have been apparent that continuing to communicate with him was not an option. If I'd taken the time to pray more and to journal about it, etc. maybe that would have helped... If I'd tried harder to find someone to reach out to, maybe that would have been more than enough... I was hard actually, even for me, to look back and understand how I let things keep going from there. I was someone who loved God passionately and was so very devoted to Him- I'd thought..! How could I have ever let myself get involved in so great a sin as an emotionally adulterous relationship with a married man?! How?! I obviously, unfortunately, had some big lessons I was still going to need to learn.

Fail

It was only maybe about a week or so later- maybe even less, when Fidel called me. And the fact is that I'd predetermined inside of myself that if he didn't respect my stated implementation of "space," and rather did try to contact me, that I would back down and take that call... I believe I was letting my own personal struggles get in the way of clarity and strength. Trying to make excuses and reasonings, rather than truly keeping truth as a top priority. I think maybe what I'd told him was that I'd pray more and see if I might have another dream showing me I could go forward in being friends with him. I think he may have already been expressing many ideas with regards to renting housing that would be used for his ministry in Israel, etc. where Believers could all live together in peace, etc.. And of course- given all the struggles I was going through at that time as far as housing was concerned- in classic narc style- his suggestions would seemingly help solve all of my most pressing difficulties. It's a classic narcissist tactic to try to make it seem like they have everything their subjects have been wanting or lacking..!!!

So I think what happened, was along the lines of this: I took time to supposedly pray about things and ended up having a dream that I tried to interpret to say I could go forward with Fidel as his friend and regarding ministry, etc. I was pretty much deceiving myself and trying to see what I wanted to see, rather than what had truly been presented to me at the start, and accepting the truth for what it was. And the fact of the matter is that not all dreams are from Above anyways- and I believe God had already clearly warned me with regards to that man. So I was being stubborn and foolish and rather than carefully keeping truth as a top priority and praying things out, etc.. I did what I wanted to do and didn't take the situation as seriously as I should have. Of course if I hadn't thought he may be one of the two witnesses- none of that may have ever come close to having happened. I think that sad deception truly had a huge impact on me wanting to keep Fidel in my life, and me feeling prompted to trust him, and feeling valuable through his acceptance, etc…

I'd really be so thankful if there was an "amazing excuse" to help make the actions that I chose at that time less serious than they were, but the fact is that the actions I chose were beyond serious! And the way I see it, is that: if I, a sincerely God-fearing and God-loving young woman found myself in an emotionally adulterous situation such as that one- how much more have other young women, who weren't so religious (or weren't religious at all!) found themselves in similar types of situations with manipulative narcissist men?!?!

CHAPTER 7: MORE WARNING SIGNS

The adulterous relationship, so-called "friendship" continued, and Fidel and I began to speak on the phone often... That would still be considered part of the "attach" phase of the narcissistic 3-part cycle, where the narcissist behaves in ways the woman may interpret as "loving"... Being very attentive, wanting to spend lots of time together, wanting to go very quickly, and so on.

Also, during the "attach" phase, by giving the woman a lot of time to speak, open her heart, and share from her thoughts- as the narcissist listens attentively to her words- the narcissist is actually employing the classic narcissistic tactic of *collecting information*. This is a "perfect" opportunity to try to learn about the woman's vulnerabilities and discover concerning the woman's "wants" and "needs." The information obtained helps give the narcissist insight concerning how he might be able to most effectively control, manipulate, and even hurt her (depending on how dark he is, so to speak...)..! It also may be used to try influence the woman to feel "addicted" to him, and dependant upon him.

Let's please clarify that "vulnerabilities" to a narcissist could literally be just about anything, so to speak. Whether on the topic of family, social life, finances, health, beauty, education, etc... Whatever the woman's story- a narcissist man may somehow try to use any one of those gathered facts against her in the future for his own perceived benefit. So it may go without saying, that individual's personal lives would typically be encouraged to be well-guarded, as far as narcissists are concerned.

Additional Warning Signs

Let's continue to review further incidents that took place with regards to Fidel, etc. that could have signaled to me that something was very wrong... While not every narc will necessarily have every single possible narc trait or standard behaviour that exists- here are some further narcissistic behaviours I believe I did find in Fidel:

1. Pressuring me at the beach.

When Fidel and I were at the beach, he pressured me to do what I didn't want to. Narcissists are predators who want to control their subjects.

2. Not taking seriously my concerns that something was wrong, etc...

Narcissists want their subjects to doubt their own perceptions, and rather to accept the narcissist's false projections and false-reality. They can perhaps be termed as absolute con artists to be on complete and unwavering guard against!

3. The exposed history of Fidel having been married 8 times.

I believe that initially Fidel hadn't been aware of what his sister had told me when we'd been at the water together and eventually, though, the topic did actually come up between Fidel and myself, with regards to his marriage history... I believe when it did, that he was not forthcoming regarding the eight marriages, and while I didn't confront him immediately about it- eventually I did inform him that his sister had said he'd been married eight times..! And I believe he may have responded with something along the lines of, that his history involved things like annulments, etc. Narcissists are typically liars, womanizers, and adulterers- and may also typically be very sexual.

For those "in the faith" marriage (as well as divorce!) is an extremely serious matter, and such a high amount of divorces and/or annulments, etc. was a huge warning signal. Actually, in all my life, I'm not sure I've ever met another human being that's been married eight times…!!!

4. I believe Fidel's sister told me that her siblings were actually warning her not to go on the trip with Fidel in the 1st place!

It may be very typical for a narcissist to have a long list of people from their past who are no longer in communication with them. While the narcissist may have their own drawn out deceptive stories with numerous false accusations against such people- the truth is that there would typically be those from the narcissist's past, such as family members, friends and colleagues, exes, etc. who have become aware of the narcissist's disordered behaviour and are threats to the narcissist's highly-prized reputation.

Please note: in a family dynamic (and otherwise…) there are many narcissists who have actually succeeded in manipulating their families, however (and others around them), and have shockingly used their enabling families, etc. to abuse and scapegoat their targeted family member, etc.

5. I believe at least some of Fidel's funding for his trips may have actually been coming from his wife!

A narc may often be a lazy user with a huge false sense of entitlement. Financially they may typically be irresponsible.

6. His supposedly good reputation.

In Fidel's past, I believe, he'd apparently worked for one of the biggest Christian tv stations in a high level position, and had been exposed to a number of rich and famous individuals from that sector... It's not rare for narcissists to, of course, want to be in or close to positions of perceived "authority" and to of course try to use that for their benefit... Some ways they may try to use such things may be: try to gain perceived "status" from those around them, to try to come across as having authority, and come across as someone worthy of trust. They may also use such things to try to control and manipulate those around them, all the more...

7. He had invited me on a trip that would take place on Shabbat, where I ended up "stuck" in a very isolating situation with him.

A classic narcissist tactic is to isolate their subject. They also may be rash and impulsive.

8. Some of his things were left at my apartment prior to the trip.

Another classic narcissist tactic is to use *entanglement*. Narcissists try to quickly entangle their lives into the lives of their subjects and try to help make it all the more difficult to get out. Already, from the start, I was "forced" to go meet him to give him his things, when otherwise I'd have seemingly surely not done so.

9. Fidel was regularly traveling between his state in USA and Israel- as well as possibly other locations.

Narcissists typically may travel a lot, something that they've used to help support them in getting away with cheating/adultery, lying, manipulating and false identities- as new environments would make leading double (or triple, etc.) lives, all the easier. They may have numerous "sides" to their personality that seem extremely different from each other.

CHAPTER 8:
IMPORTANT TOPICS

Spiritual abuse was a very significant factor in this story, that I'd be amiss not to take note of. To try to help put things into better perspective on the matter, I'd like to relay from a story I somewhat recently heard shared about online, by a man who's been viewed as a "spiritual leader," so to speak. I apologize in advance if I don't relay it 100% but I think it may have went something like this: There had been a devoted Christian couple he'd known who were part of an organization that he himself had used to be a part of- but had since left.

The organization had an event planned, which was something that perhaps didn't happen very often and that would cost the couple what to them was a significant amount of money in order to attend. They saved up for the event and perhaps regarding the money they had available and/or childcare considerations- they decided that it would end up being a "special gift" for the wife alone, and she would be the one that would "get" to attend the event while her husband would be the one to stay home...

The event was going to be several days and the wife was going to have to travel in order to get there. Well the event came and went but meanwhile the husband's very sweet and soft-spoken wife returned from the event and something was simply not right. Actually, to the contrary- something was incredibly wrong! While she had been alone at the event without her husband there helping to look out for her, the leadership acted as predators and saw her as a "target," taking advantage of her gentleness and trust. And so, as she did not have her husband there to guard and protect her, as she was used to- they managed- with their "spiritual authority" to influence and manipulate her to allow them to sexually assault her.

This would be just one example of the utterly real existence of spiritual abuse and how people with supposed "spiritual author-ity" have influenced others- even "Godly people" to allow or take part in things they otherwise would absolutely not have. Spiritual abuse was a very very factor in what took place with regards to Fidel and had he not manipulated me to think he might be one of the two witnesses I think he may have stood no chance in influen-cing me- an extremely devout God-loving individual- to fall for his act.

Codependence

Another very significant factor regarding my story, is the import-ant matter of codependence. This is not meant to be an in-depth or thorough look at what codependence is, or all the possible ap-proaches to finding complete healing concerning it- but hopefully there is, at least, a good amount of helpful information to be found here on the topic.

And of course, to please reiterate, I do share everything as a stu-dent and not a teacher, and cannot be responsible for anyone's choices or results. All decisions with regards to these things should be made with the supervision, support and full oversight of a government-approved specialist who will only be of good service. Thank you.

Those who have grown up with any type of shortage, whether serious and abusive or not, may have been at risk of develop-ing codependence. Codependence has influenced many to allow themselves to be misled by narcissists. Oftentimes, those with codependence have found themselves somehow getting into one abusive relationship, after the next. If you have been in repeatedly abusive relationships and hadn't already done so, then I'd encourage you to- God willing- consider learning more about codependence, as well as becoming very familiar with what the typical narcissist traits are, in order to help guard against ever going through another abusive relationship again!

When first hearing about codependence, many people may not have thought, at first, that it applied to them, because the label may actually be quite misleading, I believe. The fact is that many extremely independent people may also have issues what is called codependence. It, therefore, may be encouraged- when looking into what codependence is- to be deeply reflective and try to get a good list of it's possible attributes from a diverse amount of quality sources. And similar to narcissism- not all codependent traits have needed to be applicable to a person in order for them to have had a codependence issue in their lives- and at the same time, not all people who have had any of the possible common codependent traits have had an actual issue with codependence.

To briefly expound about what codependence actually is: codependence involves a lack of self-love and an unbalanced desire for the approval of others. That desire may be very deeply hidden, and even unconscious- and it may take careful and quiet reflection for someone to realize it's presence. Often those who have struggled with codependence, may have been the types who have been very eager to want to help with or fix a situation where help was "needed." They may be considered to be particularly caring, giving, and self-sacrificial people. They may feel a very large void in their lives with a deep desire to feel loved, which has made them susceptible to narcissists who specialize in acting like they will be the answer their subject has been "waiting for."

While those with codependence and narcissists are extremely different, including, of course, in romantic relationships- one commonality those with codependence actually do share with narcissists, is that they themselves may also want things to go quickly. Those with codependence may even get married or move in with someone, without first having taken the time to truly get to know them well, or really being sure that it was what they were meant to do...

While this is not a full list, whatsoever- other possible traits of codependence may include: struggling to make decisions, feeling stuck, settling, seeking to find love and validation from someone else or others, feeling invisible, being overly self-critical, and finding it difficult to say no.

Addressing Codedendence And Trauma

Anyone who has struggled with codependence, has perhaps had false messages sent towards them in their life (whether intentional or not) that belittled their value. There are many approaches and techniques that may be excellent, that can be used to help support those who've been overcoming codependence. Again, this list may not be exhaustive or go into full detail, but, depending one one's circumstance, I do think there may be some excellent and valuable suggestions found here, that I do hope would be of benefit..

Prayer

I'd like to please note from the start that prayer is, in fact, backed by science and has a number of scientific studies that do support it! I believe that sincere, truth-seeking and humble prayer may be one of the most valuable things a person could ever possibly do in their life, no matter who they are or where they are at. That being said, it is encouraged to incorporate sincere and well-intended prayer into one's daily life, praying every day. Even if a person was not sure of Who God was, God can see if a person is intending to turn to The One True Creator of the heavens and the earth.

If anyone is wondering "what is prayer?" or "how do I pray?"- I believe there are a number of different ways to pray which may all be excellent! Whether praying while literally in bed upon waking up and before going to sleep, praying on one's knees on the ground (which I do think may potentially have something that may specifically be very special about it...), praying while walking around inside one's living quarters, praying while walking outside... praying out loud, or praying in silence...; actually, on the topic of prayer, one of the verses in The Holy Bible states:

Pray without ceasing.

1 Thes 5:17 AKJV, The Holy Bible

So, my encouragement, if a person is interested in beginning to pray- is to God willing- just pray..! As a person spends time in prayer they may find themselves becoming more discerning of God's Spirit and that they are better able to discern His will. I believe they may likely also, as they continue in His Word and in prayer, find that they are making better decisions in their lives, which may likely help them get to the places they've wanted to be..!

Mindfulness

To help address codependence, a person may want to keep diligently aware of their thoughts and beliefs. If someone- in the process of overcoming codependence- was to find themselves thinking something wrongful about themselves or being overly harsh against themselves or others- to not just let the thought pass by as "acceptable," but rather to address it and expose it as false. They might want to also ask themselves where the thought might have originated from, and if something had happened in the past that had influenced them to think in such a manner against themselves or others...

Declarations And Programming

Something that may be connected to prayer, is making "declarations;" declaring truth and blessings and healing over one's life and soul, etc. Amazing scientific data has been uncovered concerning the connection between genes and programming. If you had not been doing so already, I'd encourage you to diligently take the time to intentionally program yourself in ways that support you in continuing to be the fullness of who God would want you to be, and fulfilling the true purpose of your life on this earth. How good for people to help further solidify in themselves who they really are and the fact that they're extremely valuable. I'd encourage finding Bible verses (The Word of God) that you can speak over your life and continue to go back to or ponder throughout the day. Words concerning how much God loves you, how valuable you are, and whatever else may help minister to you..

For I know the thoughts that I think toward you, saith Y-HWEH, thoughts of peace, and not of evil, to give you an expected end.

Jeremiah 29:11, The Holy Bible

For as the rain cometh down, and the snow from heaven, and returneth not thither, but watereth the earth, and maketh it bring forth and bud, that it may give seed to the sower, and bread to the eater: so shall my word be that goeth forth out of my mouth: it shall not return unto me void, but it shall accomplish that which I please, and it shall prosper in the thing whereto I sent it.

Isaiah 55:10-11, The Holy Bible

So if someone had, for instance, been "spoken down to" concerning any area of their life or self when they were growing up, they could go ahead and find Bible verses to program themselves with, to specifically help support them in believing the truth on that exact topic. Oftentimes if a person has needed to overcome codependence, it may be very wise to try to find Bible verses to help show the truth of their great value. Whatever the topic a person may want to address, the Bible has the answers. A person can speak and declare them, listen to them on audio, sing them, spend time memorizing them, write them out (-even create petitions), repeat them over and over in their head- and hopefully also help get those Bible verses deep into their heart. Using The Word of God to pursue intentionally programming one's genes, and "build oneself up" is a highly valuable practice, beyond words, and that Word is not like anything else..

Self-Care

1. Affection- Another approach that may be of support- as there is also something to be said scientifically about physical touch- is for people to literally take the time to love themselves by giving themselves long hugs on a daily basis; and while doing so, to check in with themselves and tell themselves that they love themselves. Because oftentimes people who've had codependency have been critical of themselves, it's important to try to break free from that and rather to be a good friend to oneself even within one's own thoughts, feelings and of course actions. When hugging oneself, one can then ask God to join in the hug and experience that as well, God willing. God is Love and man is precious to Him. He loves human beings tremendously... We are all His creation, after all. I hope that's encouraging.

2. Focus- On the topic of self-care, another- perhaps less frequently noted way- of taking good care of oneself is being aware of where one puts their focus. Even if a person was going through a difficult season of life- while it may be good to most certainly acknowledge that and allow oneself to process that emotionally- they also may want to be diligent to not allow that to be their main focus in their life. And to continue to keep in mind that they are blessed! Even what may seem like the most "basic" things- such as the sun having risen that morning! Continuing to focus on one's blessings can be an excellent practice to include in one's life!

3. Joy & Laughter- These are absolutely not to be underestimated and are amazing gifts from Above to most certainly seek to have incorporated into one's life. And conscious effort can very much be made regarding these things. I remember once in college having a teacher who encouraged, over time, creating a folder of images or otherwise, that made the person laugh. She talked about how whenever she was in a "bad mood" she would refer back to the compilation she, herself, had created- and how sometimes the first few images wouldn't really provoke her to laughter- but as she'd continue to look through the compilation, eventually she'd finally begin to laugh and be very much uplifted.

Laughter has of course been scientifically proven to be a very supportive behavior, and so I'd definitely encourage going along with that teacher's encouragement and compiling a tasteful and hilarious compilation of videos, memes, quotes, etc. to have available as one more tool in the tool-box, so to speak! Other ways to help support experiencing joy and laughter, can include doing the things the person enjoys the most, spending time with loving and supportive friends and family, listening to uplifting faith-based songs, and the list goes on!

4. Gifts & Special Treatment- Whether someone is single or not, that does not change how nice it might be for them to receive regular gifts (no matter how small!) and special treatments! Whether writing oneself a loving card or letter helping to build oneself up, or whatever may be suitable- being sure to take good care of oneself in such ways can be an amazing feature to include in one's lifestyle!

> *What? know ye not that your body is the temple of The Holy Spirit which is in you, which ye have of God, and ye are not your own? For ye are bought with a price: therefore glorify God in your body, and in your spirit, which are God's.*
>
> *1 Corinthians 6:19-20 *edAKJV, The Holy Bible*

The Crying Method (3-Step Process)

If someone had been carrying pain, whether from things recent or things long ago, and it was something that would be suitable for them to seek to address- I believe that a top approach in healing from it, may be to consider implementing *The Crying Method.*

This Is A 3-Step Method & Involves:

1- Prayerfully releasing that pain through crying.

2- Forgiving all involved parties, including oneself and including God (even though God is 100% innocent, sometimes a person may have perceived He had not been there for them...).

3- Giving God the burdens.

Lastly- In some cases, it may be appropriate to also pray for justice in The Name of The Messiah Y-hoshua Ha'Mashiach Jesus Christ. Very careful and accurate discernment would be required in order to know if it would be suitable to include this prayer, in whatever the circumstance was that was being addressed.

Additional Legal Disclaimer: All I share is as a student not teacher. The Crying Method and Writing Method are not necessarily for everyone and full responsibility would be upon the user to have a government-approved professional offering full legal oversight, approval, authority, and responsibility. We take the stance that sometimes leaving a traumatic past in the past may be the right choice, and that digging into the past may actually not be the best option. That decision, along with how one would choose to address their past if they did want to do so-again, are decisions that the individual would have to make with those government-approved professionals. To again reiterate- we cannot be responsible whatsoever for anything with regards to these Methods or anything else regarding this book, persons, or business, etc. Thanks..!

Pain is actually something that can be physically released through the body in the form of crying- utilizing the act of crying as a literal God-given tool..! People's hearts, minds and souls matter! If someone had been hurt in the past in a way that had not yet been fully resolved- that person is worth taking the time to acknowledge those hurts and letting themselves release that pain through crying, forgiving, and giving their burdens to God..!

With regards to the topic of carrying pain, many people may not be aware of the power of releasing that pain through crying. Many may have even felt trained to hold in their tears, and not release them at all. Often that has perhaps led to issues that would have been very easily avoidable, had they only known that crying to release that pain was an amazing option available to them. Some people may be more used to crying than others, and as it is actually a highly valuable skill, it is something to literally practice and seek to be good at.

When using prayerful crying as a tool to release pain and support personal well being, it is also important to keep oneself in the right place without veering too far into self-pity. A person should never be crying from a place of hopelessness, as there is always hope. Sometimes having pity, even for oneself, may be a good thing- but a person would want to be careful that self-pity was not something that was being dwelled upon or overly experienced, whatsoever When using *The Crying Method*, it is important for a person to accurately discern that their crying was constructive and truly coming from the right place. "Constructive crying"- at least in a way- feels good! And especially after the pain is released, there should be a very real feeling of relief.

There may, of course, be circumstances where a person may need to accept being in a situation they would prefer not to be in; and in those types of situations- while *The Crying Method* may be extremely helpful and beneficial, they may especially also want to examine some of the additional supportive options listed in this chapter to help them with accepting and getting through that circumstance in the best way possible. Enduring through hardships has been under-rated by the world, but is a very special and valuable accomplishment.

Whether a recent event, or something from decades ago, if a person was still carrying pain that had not yet been appropriately released, the negative impact could vary. It may result in extreme sadness and depression; it may result in destructive behavior and addictions; it may result in anger issues... and the list goes on. A person also may be in a place where those memories would be better left unaddressed for the time being. It may take a lot of prayerful and careful discernment to help determine what season of life a person was in, with regards to those things. If a person did find themself in a season where addressing a traumatic memory or event would be the best path for them- while there may be several ways to release pain and crying may not be the only effective option in existence, I do believe that generally speaking, that this 3-Part Method can be a #1 option to pursue.

That being said, if a person was going to be pursuing this Method, they would also want to not only be sure they truly were in a place where they were ready to face those painful memories, and acknowledge ways they'd been hurt- but to also be ready to face if there were ways they, themselves, had mis-stepped. It could take a lot of courage and depending on the amount of pain- it could also take some time. So a person would definitely want to be aware of these things in helping to determine if using *The Crying Method* might be suitable for them.

If a person was going to be pursuing this Method, in addition to having the right professional support around them, it may also be strongly recommended to be in a safe, comfortable environment, and even season of life... If a person knew about what exactly was upsetting them, then prayerfully addressing that and being willing to acknowledge the specific ways they felt hurt, may be a next step. For example, if a painful event had taken place that caused pain, then examining the specific way the hurt was felt- such as, if the person felt betrayed, mistreated, or rejected, etc. may be important to specifically acknowledge and release pain concerning.

There may be several layers, so it may be good to continue to prayerfully seek to discover all of whatever may have still needed to be released.

It may also be very good to try to remain very aware- when addressing past memories- whether through *The Crying* or *Writing Method* (more below on that!), that, of course, what took place was in the past and is thankfully not part of the present. After the Method is completed- it may be strongly suggested to try to very much "reconnect" with the present and the fact that it's a *positive* atmosphere. Taking a relaxing walk in nature, playing with one's pets, or taking a hot shower may all be ideas of ways to help support a person in that. And of course, not to be overlooked- is joy and laughter! Listening to uplifting faith-based songs, doing the things that a person enjoys the most, watching the video clips or other media compilations that make them laugh the hardest... Laughter is absolutely one of mankind's best friends in this life, there's no doubt about it.

As far as addressing trauma- perhaps someone felt something was "off" but wasn't sure what may be affecting them. They might literally want to stop and ask themselves, as well as God Elohim, "why am I feeling this way?" By seeking the answer in such a manner, they may think of the answer within moments- or perhaps later on it may come to them... They may even have a dream from Above where they are given the answer. While I do not believe all dreams are from Above- I do believe they most certainly can be. So that being said, a person may want to seek to very carefully and prayerfully discern with accuracy what to think about the dream... Sometimes, people may release pain through crying and not even be sure of the exact reason for the tears- which may also be perfectly fine! In a circumstance like that, the point may just be- to get it out!

As a person faces certain things that have hurt them, they may find that they must truly want and be willing to face the truth, and "go deep." They may have to be willing to diligently dig and explore, and be open to continuing to find things that need to be addressed. They may find that after prayerfully facing one thing and releasing pain from that, they get to a next layer, and have further realizations and tears to be cried. It is taking that time to acknowledge and validate their feelings- prayerfully feeling them out- forgiving, and giving those burdens to God Elohim (and leaving them with Him!)- that is what the 3-Step Method is all about.

Depending on the amount of pain carried, how much time a person may need to dedicate to implementing this Method and releasing pain through crying, may vary. It may take minutes, hours, weeks, or maybe even more, to get all that pain out. The good news is, that even if a person did need a bit of time to get to all of it- the positive results should still be quite immediate, and profound. Depending on how much pain they needed to release, and how much time they were finding to give themselves to address that pain- they may discover within just the first few days or weeks, that they've achieved huge and remarkable personal breakthrough... Literally each moment spent releasing pain through crying may bring noticeable breakthrough and relief.

Once something has been "felt out," if it seems a person has done all they can do by way of tears- the next step is to forgive. Before explaining further, I'd like to clarify from the beginning that forgiving someone for doing wrong, does not say that what they did was okay, whatsoever. It does not enable them or validate their actions to any extent. Additionally, it may be really good to clarify that forgiveness and trust are not the same thing. So, all of that being said- yes- forgiveness is extremely important for one's own personal well being. Whether looking at it from a purely scientific standpoint, or otherwise- there is just no way around it...

Forgiveness Tip: A way to really help be sure that someone is forgiven, I believe, is if a person is able to pray for the person they are forgiving. If they are able to pray for that person, then that may really help establish on a profound spiritual level that the forgiveness has been achieved...

Something else I'd like to please share about forgiveness is a saying I've come across that went maybe something like this: "oftentimes, when holding unforgiveness against someone, the unforgiven party either doesn't know, or doesn't care." I believe that saying helps to illustrate the fact that oftentimes unforgiveness may mainly affect the person carrying it, alone..! The sad truth is that unforgiveness has perhaps actually greatly hindered a lot of people in a variety of areas of life- including physically, spiritually, professionally, personally, and so on. But with forgiveness, there is personal freedom and huge potential for exponential growth and profound progress. It is when walking in forgiveness that a person is set up for the success of truly discovering their fullest potential, which is in Christ Jesus Messiah Y-hoshua. When people sincerely forgive others in their hearts, they are actually giving themselves a gift money can't even buy.

To briefly elaborate even further on the topic of forgiveness and it's importance, looking at things beyond this life and from more of a "big picture" standpoint- all people (including myself!) have "missed the mark," and while some may have missed it more than others- the fact is, that no one has ever done everything 100% perfectly at all times; Thus we've all been in need of God's forgiveness... So, as we all would want God to forgive us for every single time we've ever mis-stepped, the Bible seems to clearly teach that we, therefore, also are obligated to forgive all those who have wronged us...

To please reiterate- that does not make what they've done acceptable by any means, and if they'd "need" to have vengeance taken upon them- it would most certainly happen..! God is Love, but He is also just, and knows everything! People are extremely precious to Him, so please know that if someone has behaved harmfully towards another- God cares..! As people who've "missed the mark" ourselves, it's not our place to take vengeance, but His alone. If someone "should" have vengeance taken upon them, it will happen. Whether it happens in this life or perhaps is reserved even until The Day of Judgement- The One True God can be trusted concerning it 100%.

If it be possible, as much as lieth in you, live peaceably with all men. Dearly beloved, avenge not yourselves, but rather give place unto wrath: for it is written, Vengeance is mine; I will repay, saith The Lord.

*Romans 12:18-19 *edAKJV, The Holy Bible*

After this manner therefore pray ye: Our Father Which art in heaven, Hallowed be Thy name. Thy kingdom come. Thy will be done on earth, as it is in heaven. Give us this day our daily bread. And forgive us our debts, as we forgive our debtors. And lead us not into temptation, but deliver us from evil: For Thine is the kingdom, and the power, and the glory, for ever. Amen. For if ye forgive men their trespasses, your Heavenly Father will also forgive you: but if ye forgive not men their trespasses, neither will your Father forgive your trespasses.

*Matthew 6:9-15 *edAKJV, The Holy Bible*

By the way, as mentioned about earlier, just because a person has forgiven, does not mean that sometimes they shouldn't actually even pray for justice, I don't believe. As a person grows in their relationship with God, they may more easily discern concerning the most suitable things to pray for. A good way to pray regarding those who have "done wrong," may be to pray that they realize the error of their ways, and sincerely repent and turn from such things. Also, that if anything had been wrongfully taken, to per- haps pray that God would restore from what had been taken, in abundance.

Some important and uplifting news on the topic of forgiveness, is that a person does not have to rely on their own strength to forgive someone. It's literally something they can choose to do, asking God to help them to forgive sincerely with their hearts. It may also be something they'd find they'd need to do numerous times- if memories were to come up over time, for instance, and if so- that could be just fine. Whatever may be needed to remain in forgiveness- whether forgiving once, or repeatedly- to just live in a state of forgiveness, continually giving if there were any burdens to God, is an incredible path to choose that does not leave room for regret... ahmen!

During the process of releasing pain through crying, and facing things head-on that had caused them pain, a person may find there to also be actions they should take. Maybe they need to communicate something to someone, and let them know what they think or feel about something. Maybe they simply need to realize someone is not as trustworthy as they'd hoped and that stronger boundaries should be put in place. Each situation may be extremely unique, and as a person would take time to pray and develop their relationship with God, God willing, they hopefully would be able to more and more clearly discern what actions they should or should not take.

Often before taking actions, it may be strongly advised to be patient, prayerful, and make decisions only when in a calm state. Remaining prayerful, being willing to wait for clarity, and seeking God for clear discernment, may also be highly advised. No matter how hurt or wronged someone has been, it may be very good and very much in one's own best interest to try to be sure that everything they do is done from a place that is rooted and grounded in love- remembering that once actions are taken, they can't be undone. It may take a lot of restraint and maturity, and it may not be the easiest path whatsoever, but it may also be the path that looking back, they will be very glad they stuck to.

Please note: With relation to prayer, there may also the subject of "spiritual warfare," that I perhaps must address. While expounding into specific details concerning "spiritual warfare" and certain types of prayers that may directly relate to it, is outside of the scope of this book- I do think it may be important to note that "deliverance" is also a very real and relevant Biblical topic; and for those who would like to be fully healed *and delivered*, then deliverance might be a topic to also investigate further, with extreme carefulness. There may, additionally, be a number of further types of prayers to pursue that may relate to "spiritual warfare" as well as inner-healing, which may be considered quite "spiritual"- such as "covering things with the blood of The Lord Messiah Jesus Christ Y-hoshua," and so on. Again, going into those things further is outside of the scope of this book, and may only relate to some of those who have committed their lives to Christ Messiah and been born-again, but I did want to also draw attention to that.

For if the blood of bulls and of goats, and the ashes of an heifer sprinkling the unclean, sanctifieth to the purifying of the flesh: how much more shall the blood of Christ, who through The Eternal Spirit offered himself without spot to God, purge your conscience from dead works to serve The Living God?

*Hebrews 9:13-14 *edAKJV, The Holy Bible*

The Writing Method

After having already incorporated the above approaches, if a person was still feeling like they needed additional support concerning addressing anything from their past, then they may want to seriously and prayerfully consider additionally including *The Writing Method* into their lives. To briefly expound on it: while in a calm and peaceful environment, writing out (not typing!) memories in detail- and at some point being sure to, ideally, re-read what was written as well... (at least by the three week mark). At the end of each writing session, I believe it may also be highly encouraged to consciously forgive those who were involved and give all burdens to God...

Humble yourselves therefore under the mighty hand of God, that He may exalt you in due time: casting all your care upon Him; for He careth for you.

*1 Peter 5:6-7 *edAKJV, The Holy Bible*

While addressing past traumas with the support of *The Writing Method*, it may be very much encouraged not to actually talk about what took place until after it's been written out and re-

read. *The Writing Method* is meant to be used to support the person in having difficult memories moved, from being "emotionally overwhelming" into the logical part of the brain or mind. While speaking about those things beforehand may risk deepening the trauma- writing them out and then re-reading them first, may allow a person to then speak much more freely...

Meanwhile, I will reiterate that I do believe when turning to prayer and crying to release pain, first, a person may find they do not "need" to write things out- or at least not as much as they might have "needed" to otherwise. I will also state that while sometimes speaking about past traumas before having addressed them in another manner- with regards to seeking inner-healing- may be suitable, in certain circumstances, even once a person has found healing, I believe it still may be better to avoid speaking about certain things. It may be good to take time to try to discern what the best approach would be in that regard, on a case by case basis.

CHAPTER 9: FINALLY STARTING TO "GET IT"

Because I had been overseas in Israel and was still in the process of trying to obtain citizenship there, I was not wanting to sign any long-term leases, which limited my possible housing options tremendously. Fidel, in classic narcissist form, expressed that he was considering the possibility of making available the "solution!" The idea was that he'd rent a space to "set up" as a ministry type of base. And then, of course, the stable housing woes I had been struggling with would be resolved. I was "enlisted"- since he was traveling back and forth to USA and/or wherever else- to try to help find that apartment.

I was moving around a lot during the time that I was in contact with Fidel, which was over a period of around 7 months- which, the vast majority of, he was not actually physically in Israel. I'd first met him very close to the time I was leaving one particular apartment which had probably been one of the most difficult experiences I faced while in Israel, with regards to the room-mate situation I'd been in. From that location, I had been supposed to help cat-sit at another apartment for the summer- however the cat-sitting plans had suddenly changed when islamic rioting had started to break out, I think perhaps in several areas across Israel, etc...

It had actually been alone at that particular apartment where I'd planned to cat-sit- when for the first time ever, I heard a "war siren" go off. I was 100% completely alone there- and literally didn't even know what I was supposed to do! Because of that area being somewhat close to where rioting had actually been taking place, etc. I determined- I think perhaps before I'd even gone ahead and spent a single night there- that I would not be able to stay. Thankfully, the lovely women whose apartment it was, and I, were able to work things out, and help for the cat was able to be obtained from elsewhere...

From there, I went to stay at a few hostels. It was the summer of the "Operation Edge" war- and there would still be several more "war sirens" to occur in Jerusalem... but, at least going forward I'd be in a more central location, surrounded by police, etc. and somewhere I felt much more safe and secure. It was perhaps a nice relief to have all of that taken care of, and know that I would not be so isolated like I had been at the cat-sitting apartment.

So it was July and I stayed at that first hostel for maybe around 1 month. As far as my living situation was concerned, I think at least for part of the time I was staying at that hostel, that I actually was not focusing on my own needs and trying to find a more suitable location to stay for myself- but was rather trying to help find something with regards to the "ministry" apartment idea- where I'd supposedly also be staying... Actually, even in June- when I'd first met Fidel- after he'd returned to USA- before I'd even left the very first apartment I'd been staying at, I'd actually already visited an apartment for him with regards to that. I visited it, reported from the findings to him, and even took photographs for him, etc., I believe, all through my phone..!

So is that right? There I was living in a hostel, and rather than fully focusing on finding something suitable for myself, I was supposedly looking to be staying in a yet-to-be-found "ministry" apartment? I may even remember feeling burdened with regards to working to try to help find that "ministry" apartment, and I think I may also recall him actually requesting of me not to focus on finding my own apartment but to rather prioritize finding the "ministry" one. Another common narcissistic trait is for them to be overly dependent on their subjects, which I'd say this particular circumstance may very much help to demonstrate.

I also recall, while saying at that hostel, that Fidel had told me he'd had a dream about me. I remember him also not wanting to really disclose what it was fully about- though I think he may have shared that it involved a bride, or wedding dress, or something along those lines. I believe I confronted him with regards to those things and told him that I thought he had feelings for me. He did, however, continue to deny that he did, and I did let it go for the time being. I think Fidel knew exactly what he was doing and while he did eventually see himself influencing me to accept having a relationship with him that openly went beyond friendship- he may have accurately discerned that if he admitted having feelings for me at that time, that I might have cut communication with him. Narcissists may tend to be quite intelligent, and may also be very calculating.

After about a month at that 1st hostel, I moved to a 2nd hostel- which is where I stayed for several more months, from around August all the way through until around October- when I finally moved to my own apartment. It was finally while staying at that 2nd hostel, after having been in contact with Fidel for a number of months already, that I started to feel more and more conviction and clarity concerning speaking to him so often on the phone, and the fact that it was not appropriate. He had also seemingly started to really begin to shift into to the 2nd phase of the narcissistic cycle, by starting to say or do things that I felt were hurtful towards me.

The 3-Part Classic Narcissistic Cycle

There may be different words that have been used to label each of the following 3 phases, but generally I think they all may point to the same types of things. These are the terms I've chosen to use to try to help define the 3 phases of the classic narcissistic cycle:

1) Attach 2) Abuse, and 3) Abandon

1. Attach: This is the 1st phase on the 3-phase narcissistic cycle, where the narcissist behaves in a way that may influence the subject to feel extremely loved, valued and treasured. The narcissist wants to spend a lot of time with his subject and go forward with the relationship at a very fast pace. He may try to project the chemistry and dynamic as being very special to him and like nothing he'd ever experienced. A "once in a lifetime" connection. He may also be very sexual.

Please be aware, narcissists often have come across as very likeable- even to "the outside world." They may try to make themselves seem like well-doers and partake in volunteer work or charitable causes. The narcissist will want to spend a lot of time getting to know the subject, and seem very attentive and interested in what they have to say. While it may have seemed to the subject like "a desirable quality"- the narcissist was actually simply in the process of trying to "win them over" for their own purposes, as well as deceptively seeking information to be able to try to help control and manipulate the subject with, at a later date.

From early on, the narcissist also seeks to entangle his life with the subject, especially financially- as money is a "favorite" tool for narcissists to try to use to control their subjects with. Perhaps they co-signed a lease together, he borrowed money from her, etc. These types of entanglements would be an attempt to try to make it that much harder for the subject to retreat and get out of the relationship fully. The narcissist overly depends on the subject and also desires for the subject to be dependant on him. He will want to come across as either a "hero" or a "victim" when sharing stories from his past, etc. Keeping a "good reputation" is a top priority for him and he may also very much want to be in a supposed position of authority and perceived status- including with regards to his career, and so on.

Oftentimes, during this phase lots of "love hormones" have been released, and it may have literally felt like a dream. The subject may have never thought she'd ever experienced a "love" so real or fabulous in her entire life. She perhaps believed the narcissist was the most loving, considerate and attentive man towards her that she'd ever met.

2. Abuse: Eventually the narcissist shows his "other side" and from the fact that he'd been putting on an act. Of course, sometimes the narcissist would behave hurtfully concerning the subject (such as speaking negatively about her and cheating on her, etc.) without her knowledge- though I do think if paying very careful attention, that the subject would see that even in her presence he was not treating her with the full respect he "should" have...

As it had been mentioned, the spectrum of how "dark" a narcissist might be can vary. Some may truly delight in causing pain to their subjects, while others haven't gone quite so far over the edge. Some possible examples of hurtful activity narcissists have often put forth include: verbal abuse, physical abuse, spiritual abuse, and psychological abuse. They are often controlling, liars and cheaters, as well as highly manipulative. Concerning the narcissist- after having been so seemingly incredibly loving and gentle, compassionate and caring- it would be like a light switch had suddenly been turned off and "all of a sudden" they simply *did not care.* They turned into a cold person, someone without love, compassion, empathy or regard for the subject's feelings whatsoever. It's like they suddenly and literally stopped being human. This obviously may have been an incredible shock to the subject to have seen the narcissist go from perhaps the "seemingly" most loving and considerate man they'd ever met to seemingly empty, cold and inhumane.

During this phase the narcissist may devalidate the subject's feelings and show absolutely zero remorse when they have caused pain or done wrong. Narcissists do not like to be criticized or "called out" on their bad behavior. They may project their own problems onto the subject and falsely accuse or wrongfully blame the subject for things she has not done, but rather things that he is guilty of! Narcissists are hypocrites. They are not into apologies or taking responsibility for their actions. Narcissistic abuse may escalate over time. If the abuse was in an escalated state, it has perhaps felt to a narcissist's subject, when being abused by them, that they were literally being spiritually killed.

Please note: If someone has found themselves in a dangerously abusive relationship there is help. There are many women's shelters to help women escape from abusive relationships and it may be strongly advised to find professional government-approved help in safely getting out of that situation.

Confronting narcissists on their behaviour has perhaps often-times resulted in them literally going into a rage. Also during this phase, the narcissist may intentionally try to influence his subject to doubt her own understanding and perception, and to rather trust him as her supposed "source of truth." He may try to play covert and intentionally deceptive mind games with her, as well as openly try to force his false version of reality onto her.

A narcissist's image is of utmost importance to him. What matters to him is *him*. While some narcissists may have come across to the outside world as humble, other types of narcissists would have come across as very arrogant and attention-seeking from the start. Regardless of which type of narcissist they are, though, both typically have huge egos and are extremely self-seeking, self-focused and have entitlement issues. They may also typically be lazy.

When it comes to narcissistic relationships- the subject has something the narcissist wants; whether it is material, status-oriented, sexual, spiritual, etc. the narcissist's goal is to "feed" off of his subject. So it may be very helpful not to underestimate the value of being a loving, caring and considerate, sensitive human being. While some things are unseen- there may be a very special "invisible" light that goes along with being that type of person, that the narcissist would very much sense!

Narcissists may use frequent travel as a way to try to help support them in constructing a double (or triple...) life for themselves. The narcissistic personality type is actually in the same personality group as what has been termed psychopathy and sociopathy- all of which may be highly connected. It may be accurate to say that while not all narcissists would be termed psychopaths, all those who've been accurately termed psychopaths, would have also been narcissists.

As, narcissists are often liars and cheaters, which we have already covered, with regards to that, it may be very useful to please take note that they typically may try to be sure to have at least one other woman "lined up" to try to "move onto" for when they get to the 3rd phase of the narcissistic cycle and determine that they have "had their fill" and are ready to move on. Another narcissistic tactic is what's commonly called triangulating, which could involve somehow getting another woman openly involved in the relationship; and if he could influence a dynamic of having the two women fighting over him- he would love that.

Obviously the "relationship" may have become very emotionally trying to the subject, and while there may have been some supposed "good times," there'd also have often been very difficult, and emotionally painful "bad times." As mentioned, typically the "bad times" in relationships with narcissists may have continued to gradually escalate, getting worse and worse with each interval. Narcissists try to normalize poor behaviour by pushing things forward in increments over time. And that being said, they may also be sure to include some good times and possibly some seemingly incredibly sweet and thoughtful acts of kindness, on a semi-regular basis- just to help continue to confuse and control their subject!

3. Abandon: Once the narcissist has "had his fill" and is ready to try to move on to someone else, he leaves the relationship, rejecting and abandoning the subject. He typically moves on really quickly, and it may also seem very sudden. The subject might find herself shocked and in a place of extreme emotional pain. Depending on how "dark" the narcissist would have been on the spectrum- influencing the subject to feel such pain and trauma, might actually be part of what the narcissist was literally trying to do- whether obvious or not. Believing that he'd caused his subject to be emotionally damaged may literally bring the narcissist that much more satisfaction and "feed," if he were to know about or even sense it.

The narcissist will often have deceptively "bad-mouthed" the subject to those around him, etc. and the subject may even find those from the narcissist's circle giving her "dirty looks," etc. having been deceived by his lies. Eventually, whether sooner or later, though, a narcissist will typically actually try to return into the subject's life by trying to revert back into the "attach" phase, and trying to deceive the subject all over again- seeking to re-begin the destructive cycle, if the subject would allow him back! All of these things may relate to why, oftentimes, those who have broken free from narcissistic abuse may be encouraged to prayerfully consider cutting all ties with their abuser, and/or drastically limiting contact with them, at least.

> *The thief cometh not, but for to steal, and to kill, and to destroy: I am come that they might have life, and that they might have it more abundantly.*
>
> *John 10:10 *edAKJV, The Holy Bible*

CHAPTER 10: NO HOPE FOR A NARCISSIST?

In the secular world, generally, many seem to be of the understanding that there is simply no hope for a narcissist. None, nil, zero. It seems that such highly manipulative individuals, for whatever reason, have gotten so "set in their ways," and despite all of their wrongs- have not experienced enough guilt, shame or remorse to actually be willing to truly and consistently pursue and experience change. Pursuing change would include admitting their wrongs, and narcissists (whose reputations are of "top priority" to them) typically do not want to admit they're the ones at fault... ever... for anything... Oh sure, once in a while, they may actually briefly feel bad about something and, yeah they will suck it up and apologize in order to serve their purposes, and when it's really just part of their game- but these things typically will simply not truly lead towards actual lasting change..!

Actually it is part of their "act" as a narcissist to typically blame and project their own wrongdoings onto others; thus it's the sad, hard truth: no matter the "treatment" and no matter how much time has gone by, such individuals not only often have remained narcissists- but their disorder has typically, if anything, become even more fortified.

Now that I've shared concerning the secular worldly view, I do have to share an even deeper truth: t\That with The Lord Jesus Christ Messiah Y-hoshua- there is hope.

> *But Jesus beheld them, and said unto them, With men this*
> *is impossible; but with God all things are possible.*
>
> *Matthew 19:26 *edAKJV, The Holy Bible*

That being said, women may need to be very careful and well aware that, with regards to the 3-phase narcissistic cycle, after a certain amount of time has passed, it may not be an uncommon what soever, for the narcissist to eventually turn right around and seek to re-begin the cycle all over again! To go back to the 1st phase, at least for enough time to win back the subject's trust- and that may include being very apologetic and acting oh so understanding! As part of this tactic, they may say that they realized they'd done wrong, and may even say they found or turned back to God..! Or whatever the story may be!

Time and again, if the narcissist had not sincerely found God, and was not genuinely committed to being who they were meant to be in Messiah Y-hoshua Jesus Christ- then generally the things they'd said and done when trying to see if they could maneuver their way back into the subject's life are just part of what would be yet another hoax.

Losing The Battle, But Not The War

To continue to relay from what took place concerning Fidel... It was when I'd been staying at that 2nd hostel that I'd started to feel more and more strongly that I should be cutting ties with or at least cutting down communication with him. I think the way things may have unfolded at that time, is: that I actually did go ahead and let him know where I stood... he had a bad reaction to that, said something that had hurt me- and *finally* I went ahead and cut communication with him.

So that was that and life went on. It had perhaps been several weeks or so since I'd ended contact with him, and I was still staying at that 2nd hostel, when one day I went downstairs and *there he was* near the hostel's front desk area. Thankfully he hadn't seen me and I think I simply dashed straight to my female dorm room; extremely upset and not sure of what to do. I honestly- other than possibly feeling stalked and disrespected by his appearance (since he knew I was staying there and that I didn't want to communicate with him), was also probably scared of falling into sin and getting sucked back into a "friendship" with him. So, perhaps without realizing it- I believe I may have actually followed what it seems The Holy Bible may teach, regarding how to handle temptation- and I fled!

Run from temptations

2 Tim 2:22a CEM, The Holy Bible

I was able to find someone I knew who lived closer to the Tel Aviv area of Israel and who'd said I could stay there for a few days, or whatever. So I made it to their place, and while I was there, I suppose I'd perhaps still been pretty freaked out. There were perhaps no other good clean hostels that I was aware of at that time, which were located in the area that I preferred to be- and so I wasn't sure what to do. The other strange thing was that before I left I did see Fidel once more- without him seeing me, and saw that he was sitting next to another older man. I somehow knew that it was one of his friends and that he was promoting the idea that this was the 2nd witness. I think I may have felt a strong push towards wanting to stay involved in the things going on and to "get to" also meet that supposed 2nd witness- as I was still seemingly under a very real level of deception- but I had thankfully determined to ignore that tug, and to just stay hidden- and get out of there!

So, once I was staying at the location near Tel Aviv- as I pondered the situation I was in, and felt a lot of distress concerning it-honestly, what I think I really may have wanted was for there to be some type of spiritually authoritative male figure in our "community" to intervene on my behalf. For him to be willing to speak to Fidel for me, and ask him to leave that hostel and respect my right to have space from him... But I, sadly, perhaps just didn't know of anyone to turn to, to do that for me. I didn't want to "have" to be the one to confront him, because I felt like that was letting him "win." It was letting him control and manipulate me into having contact with him, rather than doing what I'd wanted, which was not to have contact. I did end up finally deciding, I believe, to go ahead and email him and ask him to leave the hostel... I believe he may have responded by writing something along the lines of, that he had already pre-paid for a number of days but once the time was expired he'd move.

And so I think it was maybe 3 or 4 days, before I returned to Jerusalem. Remaining where I'd been located near Tel Aviv no longer seemed to be much of an option, so my plan was to try to find an apartment in Jerusalem ASAP. By the time I arrived back in Jerusalem, I believe I'd already had it scheduled to go visit an apartment- and I think I was actually hoping to be able to "close the deal" very quickly, even that very day, if possible- and that it would of course hopefully be a good place for me. The way things turned out was that I did go to see that apartment and I did close the deal very quickly; however I think I still was forced to wait a day or so before I could move in... So, as I still seemingly had not come up with anywhere else to go that I would feel "secure," etc. I ended up staying at the hostel for just one more night or so.

I guess it was during that time, I did somewhat get that male assistance that I'd wanted. I think it was morning time and I was in the cafeteria area of the hostel talking to some of the Christian volunteers that I knew, and actually I think relaying to them from some of the situation that had been taking place... That some married man who I'd tried to cut ties with had shown up at the hostel- and how distressed I'd been over it, or whatever. And I believe it was literally as I was sitting there with them, after having told them about some of the things I'd been going through- when Fidel showed up in that very cafeteria area and actually began to try to speak to me! But I was not wanting to see him, so I think I pretty much just tried to ignore him, and got up and walked away... I ended up on the other side of the vicinity when I think once again he continued to try to approach me... It was at that time that one of those male Christian volunteers named Michael intervened and told him maybe something along the lines of: "Leave her alone. She doesn't want to talk to you."

Well, thankfully, I wasn't going to be staying at that hostel for much longer and it wasn't long before I was out of that bizarre situation, and had signed the contract for the apartment I'd found. It met my stipulations, and I'd be able to rent it on a month-to-month basis, giving 30 days notice if I'd be leaving. Not much time had passed, and it was already getting close to the Day of Atonements that year- which was the time of year it may be all the more emphasized for people to want to be at "peace" with others, etc. I was doing well and had been keeping full distance from Fidel since having left the hostel, but then I found myself get slightly off track again... It seems I just didn't really fully understand how serious of a situation I'd encountered and how fully I should really be keeping my guards up with regards to that man.

So, unfortunately, I think I actually may have started to let myself feel "guilty" regarding some of the things that had happened, since Fidel had arrived in Jerusalem, etc. Maybe specifically the email I'd sent him when I'd been staying near Tel Aviv that I may have thought had been somewhat cold or stern, etc. And so not wanting to be in a "conflict" and feeling eager to not be on "bad terms" with anyone that time of year, specifically- I did determine to send him another email, where I think I may have pretty much apologized if I'd done anything wrong and tried to make so-called "peace." It's not that I was jumping back into making plans with him or talking to him on the phone again, by any means- but it was still a step that I personally don't think needed to be taken, and that shouldn't have been taken.

Meanwhile- that was that, and "life went on." The unfortunate circumstance was that he was still going to be in Israel for a while longer- and downtown Jerusalem was not the biggest place, by any means... So, that being said, the chances of me running into him were seemingly going to be quite high if he was going to keep hanging around in Jerusalem. The apartment I was renting was downtown, and with the war that had just passed- being central was something that may have helped me to feel more"secure." So if Fidel was going to be in Jerusalem for a while, and if I wasn't looking to move again, then knowing that running into him was not going to be out of the question, was something I was just going to seemingly have to learn to "deal with."

All of that being said- it probably didn't even take a week before I did run into him- on my very street. As we were now "on good terms"- we spoke for a bit and I think he was, once again, trying to talk to me about the idea of me working with him, to help in the "ministry" work he was supposedly planning to do there, etc.. But I believe my response was along the lines of- that I didn't feel I'd been clearly shown from Above to do so, and unless I did receive that clarity, the answer was no. After maybe a few minutes or so of talking, I went on my way and the conversation was over.

Meanwhile, I had a friend named Daniel who was volunteering on a kibbutz in southern Israel that I'd occasionally visit with. I'd actually met him, when a while prior- I'd briefly volunteered on a farm in northern Israel... We'd gotten along really well when I was there, and during that time, I'd actually been used from Above to help lead him to giving his life to Messiah and being born-again! So, anyways, we'd arranged that he'd come visit Jerusalem and stay with me for a few days or so. During our short visit, as we were approaching the end of his trip- we ended up going into Jerusalem's Old City. As we were getting ready to head back to the downtown area, I was waiting for him outside of an Old City store, as he was busy buying something... I think it may have been fresh juice, if I recall correctly! As I was waiting for him- I "unexpect-edly" saw Fidel around the corner from the store- not so far away.

However- he didn't see me.

My friend Daniel knew who Fidel was- but had never actually met him. After seeing him, I think my first reaction was to quickly walk back towards the store where Daniel was and remain hidden behind that corner... So that's what I did... But sadly, it regrettably wasn't so long before I actually felt tempted to walk up back to Fidel to say hi- and introduce him to my friend Daniel. Obviously, at that time, I still didn't fully understand who Fidel was, and who Fidel wasn't. And so, yes- that still probably of course had a huge influence on how I perceived him. But clearly looking back it was so obvious there was something seriously wrong with him and the situation- and I really, really feel I should have known better. So I do feel immense regret looking back at this and yet of course there's no way for me to go back and change what happened, as much as I'd want to be able to do so. So once again, with regards to dealing with narcissists- I was going to learn something the hard way.

I updated Daniel regarding having seen Fidel around the corner, and asked him if he wanted to meet him. I then proceeded to allow Fidel to see us, and introduced them to one another. Fidel then informed us that he was about to lead a meeting with other Believers he'd met, in around 30 minutes or so- and invited us to join the meeting. He told us where it would be- but we decided decline... After Daniel and I had said our goodbyes and were on our way back to my place, I once again began to feel tempted, and wanted to attend the meeting... I talked to Daniel about it and, that being said, we actually ended up turning right back around, and heading to the location where it was supposed to be held.

We arrived at the meeting and ended up being a group of maybe around 10 people, both men and women- though I do think it may have actually been predominantly ladies... I believe that Daniel and I actually arrived before Fidel- who, as we had declined the invitation- was not expecting us to be there... So in classic narcissist form he actually literally showed up- with yet one more young woman! This guy was no joke! And on top of that... I really don't know how he did it... but it seemed this entire group was looking to him as their "leader," and that even some of them were of the impression that he was one of the two witnesses! I also remember Fidel trying to portray to the attendees concerning how "special" of a person I was, or whatever...

While Daniel and I had still not met Fidel's friend- that other supposed "witness"- I think just about everyone else at that meeting had perhaps already met him... I'll call him Frank. And yes, Fidel's friend Frank was also going by a Hebrew name to those around him... I'd imagine having the two of them there may have made Fidel that much more convincing regarding who he was portraying himself to be; because, as I'd mentioned, Fidel had worked at one of the biggest Christian tv stations in USA for a season, and been exposed to some of those "rich and famous" in the mainstream Christian world. Figures that he seemingly may have been trying to "expose"- with regards to this, that, or the other. And so the fact that his friend Frank had actually apparently also worked there with him... and actually had a congregation in USA where he was a "spiritual leader"... yes- I guess that surely must have helped Fidel be all the more convincing! But I was still so deceived at the time I think I actually felt disappointed that Frank wasn't at the meeting for me to have the "honor" of meeting him!

To please note: I do want to please be clear that it was seemingly much more Fidel who was wanting to push the doctrine of them potentially being the 2 witnesses. His friend Frank, on the other hand, ended up not being quite as determined regarding it, and seemingly did at least eventually express doubts regarding it.

The Fall

It was only maybe just around 48 hours from that meeting, when Fidel contacted me on my cell phone regarding supposed drama that had taken place at the hostel where he'd been staying. Apparently he was feeling physically threatened, or whatever, and needed a place to stay that night. I think it may have been pretty late and that hostels had been quite filled up, so somehow I ended up feeling inclined by him to let him stay at my place! Obviously, this clearly from an outside perspective, might seem like it could be an absolute disaster waiting to happen! And regrettably, that's exactly what it turned out to be!

Yet, somehow, after having no incidents with my friend Daniel who had just left- I think I may have just foolishly hoped I could offer Fidel that same amount of trust. I, also for some reason, think I might have failed to see past his story and recognize that despite it being late at night- there had to be somewhere else for him to go- and my place was simply not an option for a married man! And not to mention, a man I had been warned in a dream, months prior- with regards to!

Well, anyways, I did end up letting him stay at my apartment that night, and from there he unsurprisingly seemingly did not want to leave! Honestly, it was obviously, absolutely ridiculous that I was letting him stay at my tiny apartment- and *totally* inappropriate! And so it is when he was staying there that things really took a terrible turn. While inside of my apartment, he continually found excuses to touch me in a "casual" way. I think maybe after a few times I told him I didn't want to be touched and asked him to please stop. He, however, of course did not respect me in that regard, and at a certain point when we were praying about something- again he tried to touch my hand during the prayer. I "called him out" regarding the touching- to which he persisted in pressuring me- that since it was for prayer it shouldn't be an issue, or whatever.

I backed down- and it was that exact incident which ended up leading to sexual immorality. At no point in history did we have "all out sex" but we did most certainly and regrettably cross the line physically multiple times during that visit, over the period of maybe a few weeks. And so, I believe it was right after that first incident, however, that he "confessed his love for me." I remember my reaction was somewhat shocked, perhaps, and I confronted him about how I'd continually suspected him of having feelings for me in past months but he'd continually denied it; and then all of a sudden he was admitting he supposedly loved me!?

My response to his "profession" was maybe more something like: that what had happened between me and him physically- as far as I was concerned- was me giving into "the flesh." I was someone who'd been "keeping myself" for a while, and was wanting to be pure until I was with whoever my real "meant to be" husband was- which even as a born-again Believer, wasn't necessarily the easiest path to follow whatsoever. So, as far as I was concerned- to have some man repeatedly touching me, etc.- it perhaps wasn't shocking that eventually "the flesh" over.

Well I think he'd already maybe been staying at my apartment for at least a few days- and I recall clearly pressing him regarding going to stay in a hostel... but he of course fought back and responded that the hostel was full... I think it may have also been around that time when he had taken things to a whole other level and said that he was actually looking to find a way to leave his wife for me! This was something that I think has probably never crossed my mind even once. So, finally after probably at least several more days if not even weeks, I gave up and pretty much forced him to leave. My stance was pretty much- you have a wife and you need to leave to go and actually act like you should with regards to that. I think I was still open to being around him if there were others there and it was a public place, but I wanted to be careful and definitely did not want to cross any more lines physically.

So, Fidel spent his 1st night back at the hostel and things were supposed to be getting straightened out, right? He was supposed to be living up to his so-called "Last Days Prophet" title and pursuing an upright walk in total faithfulness to his wife that he'd left back in USA. Right.. I don't think he lasted 1 day! Actually, I believe it was that very next morning at his hostel that he apparently...

met someone! And he spent the whole day with her showing her around Jerusalem, too! I think he may have tried to say that it was platonic and that he had even talked about me throughout the day but, obviously, as much as I didn't understand, I did know that he was someone who was very much capable of being involved in romance outside of his marriage.

I must have been so confused, because on the one hand I thought he might be some incredibly special human being and I felt so privileged to have the opportunity to "be in his circle"- yet on the other hand, his actions were what some may label as appalling! I think I might have somehow reasoned to myself that even those called to ministry may have weaknesses, but, I'd just gotten so wrapped up into things- I wasn't recognizing the severity of what had happened or what was happening. Aka, adultery. Aka, 10 commandments. Aka, one of the biggest sins a human could commit. I learned a lot after everything finally was over and my boundaries with married men are no joke, but at the time, it seems I still had a lot to "get together" and even with regards to the reality of "emotional adultery" just had so much to come to terms with.

So, anyways, he really did choose the perfect tactic to mess with me, by spending that day with that girl, in the way that he did. He really did. Because, unexpectedly- after having thought that what had happened with him was something that had been very much in "the flesh" and that my feelings had not really been so involved... I did realize that something had shifted at least at some point, and I did, regrettably, feel jealous. Actually, when they were together, I remember feeling extremely upset and even distressed! I remember feeling like- I sent him out of my apartment for him to be a good husband for his wife. Not so he could go off with someone else! Triangulation was mentioned earlier in this book and just to reiterate, it really has been a very effective tactic that narcissists have used and so it most definitely should ideally not be underestimated.

So, the drama continued to unfold, and while I think during that time I was really struggling concerning what boundaries to set and keep, etc. As far as if I would be alone with him in public, sort of thing, etc. I think maybe especially with connection to me not wanting him off with another female, I did continue to make compromises and ended up sinning with him physically a few more times, before he was finally to leave Israel and go back to his house in USA. But to please be clear, regarding the two "events" during that period, where I remember lines being crossed in that manner- he was playing a major role. I remember him literally using force when he was outside of my apartment, which really should have been enough for me to finally cut ties with him. But then there was once again the 2nd event where I somehow allowed him to pressure me to go on a day trip with him and while we were there, I think he may have once again been trying to force himself on me.

I remember we were supposed to be returning to Jerusalem and he was, meanwhile, trying to convince me to stay at a hotel with him. I remember sitting outside of the hotel at the bus-stop trying to reason with him regarding why we were not meant to be romantically involved and then finally him caving and saying he understood and agreed with me. I fell for it and did finally give in and agreed to stay at the hotel- and then of course he totally flipped after a short while and once again wanted to be romantically involved. Looking back, it really is ridiculous that I actually thought he may have given up on the idea, but again I think the fact that I still seemed to think that he might be some "Great Prophet" really made it harder for me to see things as they were. And somehow I just kept allowing myself to be sucked in by him.

CHAPTER 11:
WINNING THE WAR,
OVER FOR GOOD

Soon after Fidel had finally left Israel, I recall hanging up on him due to his behavior that was clearly going beyond a so-called "friendship." I think I may have ended up, pretty much deciding that I was going to be taking space from him and just didn't really want to be in a lot of communication for the time being- if any at all. I also think I may have made it very clear to him that all romance was over for good. But I still, for some reason, seemingly thought I could possibly help serve in his so-called upcoming "ministry," and thought we could still be "friends."

I was starting to finally realize that what had happened was very bad, and I remember being so upset and concerned, and praying and asking God something like- if He agreed and saw that I was pressured and influenced by Fidel with regards to the adultery that had taken place? After prayerfully seeking God regarding that, I did have a dream, I think maybe that very night, that I do believe was from Above. It went maybe something like this: I saw Fidel had pressured and influenced me to stay out late so that I then ended up needing to take the bus home alone late at night in an area it wasn't the safest to do so. I also saw in the dream that he hadn't realized or known about the danger he'd influenced me to put myself in (if God wouldn't have been protecting me...)- but that didn't change the fact that he had influenced me in such a manner.

Narcissists may be quite reckless, lawless, impulsive, and of course selfish. While some narcissists may be very sadistic, and derive pleasure through causing harm to others, I don't believe Fidel's main goal with regards to the adultery was to try to "harm me." I think his intentions were more along the lines of, simply seeking to serve whatever it was that he felt he wanted at that time, for himself. How it might have negatively impacted my life or the lives of anyone else around him- to him- I don't believe was even something he'd put careful consideration towards.

So with regards to that dream, I felt like God was confirming to me that, yes, He did see that I had been pressured and greatly influenced by Fidel to partake in so great a sin as adultery- which was so far from anything I had perhaps ever seen myself taking part in as the devoted born-again Believer that I was! Just to reference it again, I was literally sitting outside reading from The Holy Bible when Fidel had 1st approached me! What happened literally knocked me on my feet and I just didn't see it coming as far as the fact that I'd have actually partaken in something so serious! I had literally put the salvation of my soul in danger (if not repented of...)! I believe the dream also helped to shed light on Fidel's possible "oblivion" concerning how dangerous adultery truly can be, with regards to how much it truly could send a person "straight to hell," if not repented of, so to speak.

Consequences Leading To Clarity?

Please note: That when I do talk about things like discipline and consequences that I believe I have received, that is my interpretation of what I think has likely happened- but I most certainly can't speak for God Y-

H of course, by any means, please! Thanks!

Within a short amount of time, I'd ended up moving to another small apartment close by. Fidel was still, thankfully, no longer in Israel- but I believe that I was about to have to pay a major price for my serious sin. Keeping in mind, that what I did- I did as a born-again Believer who knew that adultery was most serious. I'd also even received a warning dream concerning him, long before things had escalated. So, by that point, as much as I had repented of- I had still had the impression that I could somehow help "serve his ministry." Once the consequences really started to take place, I did quickly realize that there was more I was going to have to do, with regards to repentance, and I was going to have to cut all lines of communication 100% for good.

So as far as the consequences are concerned... to get straight to the point of what happened... It had seemed I'd ended up accidentally ingesting some toxic chemicals over a period of several days, or even possibly over a week. On top of that, as it turned out- the government trained regular MD doctors had not seemed to have received thorough training in herbalism, etc. and were not even close to well trained or educated in helping me to fully heal from the poisoning, it my opinion! It would have possibly been a complete and utter disaster if it had not been for, I believe, God Y-H having been there for me, and me having received lots of direction and help from Above regarding what treatment to pursue. I believe I was clearly shown many things to do in dreams, and also very blessed to get to meet online with an MD who was knowledgeable in herbalism and who confirmed from the information I had received.

Even before I'd realized I had entered into a time of serious discipline, I believe I'd received very comforting and assuring communication from Above that had helped me to feel extremely secure, that God Y-H had not forsaken me. So- I was blessed to have that peace as I was going through that, thankfully; because otherwise... I really think I may have been so terrified that He'd completely rejected me, that I'm not sure how I'd have beared it! After King David had been in adultery with Batsheva, I believe it took a Prophet sent by God showing up and speaking to him, for him to truly "wake up" concerning his wrongs. (2 Samuel, Chapter 11 and 12.)

For me, I believe it was the above incident that was not only- in part- me paying a price for, and receiving discipline for the sins I'd committed- but also that was meant to be used to help get me to "wake up" concerning further steps I'd still needed to take, if I'd truly wanted to repent fully. Just cutting down on communication and supposedly "ending the affair" would not have been enough, I don't believe. Ties had to be fully cut and doors to the idea of me possibly helping support his "ministry" needed to be fully closed, for once and for all- whether he was a so-called "famous Last Days Prophet" or not!

Around that time, I'd also confessed of my sins to a few ladies I'd been in contact with- which I also think was perhaps a pretty important thing to have taken part in. Even before the poisoning had taken place, I think I may have partaken in *some* of that confession- however, I still had not accepted that I needed to cut all ties and close all doors 100% forever. But finally, I believe it was not so long after the poisoning had taken place, that I finally started to really "get it" more fully and see that "being friends" or "working" with Fidel was simply not an option. Whether or not he was one of two witnesses- it didn't matter- being in communication with him was just was not going to be an option for me, period.

I also did not realize it right away, but I think there may have also been longer-term consequences regarding the affair that took place. I will note that while at the time I was still somewhat of a "newer" Believer- I did seemingly have a very real prophetic gifting and am someone who *is* actually called to ministry- I believe. And so I do think that that may mean that while the enemy may have been seeking to "go after me" all the more to try to cause me to stumble- the discipline I need to be ready to receive, at times, if

I do mis-step- may be very serious, indeed. And given the severity of the sin and the fact that I was even warned from Above beforehand regarding it... the price that I was going to have to pay was going to be heavy.

But I accept that. I was so surprised looking back on it because I felt like it almost was something that had happened to me. Because I just didn't expect to have been through something like that. So it's a bit complicated and while on the one hand I do and must take responsibility for my wrongs and accept that God Y-H had every right to expect more from me... I also know that He knew I was going to mess up and that there were still things I was going to need to learn before I would get to a place where if put in that type of situation again, things would be handled incredibly differently. If that's how to put all of that.

So that being said, not only did I go through that initial ordeal that took place that helped me finally "wake up" and seek to really, fully repent. But thereafter I also think God Y-H may have allowed me to make a poor choice to leave Jerusalem and move south, with regards to me needing to face even further discipline. And from there I actually ended up having probably the hardest year of my life, as a born-again Believer! And I ended up also losing that battle for citizenship in my country, Israel! So, talk about repercussions that it seems I may have faced truly all because of things that happened with Fidel! Because I do not know for sure, by any means, but I definitely do think that if I had made better choices regarding Fidel, that I may have actually won that case I'd been fighting all those years.

But once again, it is what it is. I trust God Y-H in every way and I know that He uses all things for good for those who love Him and are called according to His purpose. He knew I was going to "mess up" before I even stepped foot in Israel and so as regrettable what happened is- I still do have the benefit- just like all of His followers- of having a compassionate God to be able to turn to who did not come to the world to condemn the world, but to save it.

And I may also interject, on another bright note, how amazingly life changing that detox was for me, as far as it being used for good in an entirely different area of my life from many years prior... As far as the fact, that by doing the very deep detox that I'd never done on that level before, I also ended up addressing some of the other things that needed to be confronted and found profound changes take place, with regards to it, that I had absolutely not anticipated! So that was incredible.

So the "relationship" was finally over for good, and while it only took place over around maybe seven months or so, and was mostly what some may term as an "emotional affair" that was taking place long-distance and over the phone- it's something I'll regret for the rest of my life. I know I can't change what happened, but what I can do, however, is be thankful that I serve a forgiving God, Who I believe has accepted me despite what I did those years ago. A God Who is not to be tested, and at the same time, a God Who is compassionate and Who is Love.

The fact is that all have sinned and fallen short and people don't always see where a person is coming from and what their intentions are when they make the mis-steps they do. So I do hope everyone will please remember to let God Y-H be The Judge and not try to hold anyone to standards that they may not truly know for sure if they'd have been able to even meet if put in the same situation. I can't say I deserved God's mercies or faithfulness after my willful disobedience and sin, but the truth is that I don't believe anyone has deserved God's forgiveness. And that being said, He's just so good that He has offered it anyways.

Being a servant of God is not about having a perfect track record, and if it was then no one would "make the cut." Rather, I believe being a servant of God Y-H includes truly wanting the truth, being willing to repent, willing to obey, and if a person has fallen- being willing to try to get right back up again, and keep pressing forward. As His servant, I do want to love Him more than anything or anyone, and keep Him as my top priority. I know that I cannot accomplish anything good apart from Him, but I also know that with God all things are possible.

If we say that we have no sin, we deceive ourselves, and the truth is not in us. If we confess our sins, he is faithful and just to forgive us our sins, and to cleanse us from all unrighteousness.

1 John 1:8-9 AKJV, The Holy Bible

And we know that all things work together for good to them that love God, to them who are the called according to His purpose.

Romans 8:28 AKJV, The Holy Bible

CHAPTER 12:
GOOD NEWS

So that's from "my story" of when I allowed myself to actually get involved in a flat out adulterous relationship with a married man. I believe I encountered a list of highly-manipulative narcissistic conduct, from a man who was older than me, and seemingly may have had lots of experience taking advantage of women- and yet I have no excuse. Whatever price I may have had to pay with reference to the poor choices I'd made, I believe is only a tiny fraction of what I truly would deserve. And the fact remains that whether "great" or "small," I believe all men have sinned and would be deserving of eternal hell fire, with the only thing making any of us worthy of Eternal Paradise being, having received the blood atonement sacrifice of The Lord Jesus Christ, Y-hoshua Ha'Mashiach.

Despite the fact that we have all sinned, God came to the earth with a part of Himself because He loves us and didn't want the enemy to succeed in bringing any of us to the eternal suffering that was actually created for the devil.

The Lord is not slack concerning His promise, as some men count slackness; but is longsuffering to us-ward, not willing that any should perish, but that all should come to repentance.

*2 Peter 3:9 *edAKJV, The Holy Bible*

Being the Perfect God that He is and yet being in a human body, He was able to overcome sin for mankind. Because He had no sin, His blood that He willingly offered, was able to make atonement for all mankind's sins. In order to receive His free gift now, a person only needs to sincerely believe in The Lord Jesus, give their life to Him 100%. It's just one sincere decision! Salvation comes by the grace (undeserved forgiveness) of God through faith in The Lord Jesus Christ, The Messiah Y-hoshua. When a person simply chooses to believe in and commit their life to Him, they receive that blood atonement sacrifice and all their sins are blotted out. They've become part of "His body" and are "born-again," receiving The Holy Spirit, and their desires change. God is The Father, The Son and The Holy Spirit; for these Three are One.

> *for all have sinned, and come short of the glory of God; being justified freely by His grace through the redemption that is in Christ Jesus: whom God hath set forth to be a propitiation through faith in His blood, to declare his righteousness for the remission of sins that are past, through the forbearance of God; to declare, I say, at this time His righteousness: that He might be just, and the justifier of him which believeth in Jesus.*

*Romans 3:23-26 *edAKJV, The Holy Bible*

Whether adultery, fornication, murder, lying, stealing, etc. whatever the sin- no matter how big and no matter how many- the Lord Jesus Christ, Y-hoshua The Messiah, paid the price so mankind wouldn't have to. I believe even if it had been just for one person that He still would have gone through with being beaten beyond recognition- and that that's how precious each soul is to Him..! So if anyone had not yet committed their life to The Lord Jesus, or had backslidden from walking that right path, etc. God Y-H willing- now is the time to "get right with God."

I believe He forgave King David for the adultery he committed (and, I believe, for successfully trying to have the woman's husband killed after he'd impregnated her...), I believe He forgave me for the adultery I committed- and for whatever you've done- I believe He would want to forgive you as well. Each soul has been given the gift of "free will" and it is up to each individual to choose to want to turn to God Y-H and commit their life to The Lord Jesus Christ, or not.

that if thou shalt confess with thy mouth the Lord Jesus, and shalt believe in thine heart that God hath raised Him from the dead, thou shalt be saved. For with the heart man believeth unto righteousness; and with the mouth confession is made unto salvation. For the scripture saith, Whosoever believeth on Him shall not be ashamed.

*Romans 10:9-11 *edAKJV, The Holy Bible*

Do I think it's possible that The Lord Jesus Messiah might appear to some unbelievers at their final moments and make available to them the opportunity to receive Him? I am not God, I wouldn't even want to try say what I think He might or might not do. But that being said, for all who are alive today, I do feel strongly that it's just not worth the risk, ideally, and giving one's life to God is not only about eternal salvation (which is beyond huge in itself of course), but also about simply doing the right thing. He is The One Who created us and Who loves us. He is The One Who makes the sun go forth every morning. Sure there's a spiritual war out there, sure the devil hates all mankind and has been doing horrible things- but that doesn't change that God is perfect and good, and has an amazing eternal paradise for those who will choose Him!

In closing, I just want to say that no temporary worldly pleasure is worth eternity in hellfire and away from The One True God, our Creator Who is Love. Please make the right choice without delay, God willing. I believe the last of "The Last Days" has very much already begun, and I've been talking about them for years... If you have a Bible, and are willing, I'd also definitely encourage you to go ahead and find the 4th book in the New Testament commonly called "The Gospel of John." That book, I believe, has been used by God Y-H to help drastically change more lives for the better, than possibly any other book in the entire world! You can also read it for free online!

If you have not yet committed your life to The Lord Jesus Christ and are ready to do so now, then I'd be honored to help lead you in a prayer with regards to that, if you'd like. If so, please read the following words out loud, as you mean them sincerely in your heart:

I, (insert name), confess with my mouth The Lord Jesus, Messiah Y-hoshua, and believe in my heart that God has raised Him from the dead, and I am saved. I believe in You, Messiah Jesus Christ Y-hoshua, and I believe that You died on the cross and were resurrected after three days and then ascended to Heaven. I give my life to You 100% and ask You to now please fill me with Your Holy Spirit as I receive Your blood atonement offering that You have given for me. I thank You for what You have done and I thank You that from this day forth I am now saved! Hallelu Y-H!

If you have truly committed your life to Him, you've literally made the best decision you could possibly make for your own soul: congratulations! As a born-again Believer you are blessed to get to have God's Holy Spirit living inside of you now, and may already feel extremely different! You will probably find that you have a a brand new very special comfort and peace. As a new believer, there will typically be a special journey of continuing to be cleansed- and it's highly encouraged to try to be in daily prayer and Bible reading. Your desires have changed so following the right path will now be a lot "easier" so to speak, so from this point it will be good to try to leave any past sinful ways in the past and continue to press forward in the good direction! As you read The Bible you can gradually learn and implement God's ways as His Spirit guides you!

There may be true "spiritual leaders" out there, but there may also be many, many false ones- so, what's most important is you having your own personal relationship with God. He has never and will never fail! I hope you're encouraged, and if this book is meant from Above to be used to accomplish any purpose, that it accomplishes it's designated purpose to the fullest. In Messiah Jesus

Christ Y-hoshua's Name and by His blood. Ahmen.

Draw nigh to God, and He will draw nigh to you.

*James 4:8a *edAKJV, The Holy Bible*

ABOUT THE AUTHOR

Jacqueline Servantess is an author, entrepreneur and is involved in ministry, which she provides on a 100% volunteer basis. She has a variety of passions and has attended schools for business, sound engineering, as well as family herbalism and wellness coaching. Jacqueline sincerely cares about people and seeks to support them in reaching their fullest potential in every way: body, soul and spirit.

She believes everyone has been uniquely designed and is greatly loved by their Maker, with a role that no one else can fulfill, and with regards to "the church"- she is disappointed that she does not believe those in "leadership" have typically been encouraging followers of Christ Messiah enough- to seek to know and live out, their God-appointed destinies! She believes this has also of course influenced the way they relate to those who have not yet committed their lives to Him.

Jacqueline is a born-again Believer in Messiah Christ Lord Jesus Y-hoshua, and also refers to herself as a "Torah-Keeper." She believes in following Messiah Jesus Y-hoshua's example more closely as far as things like resting on God's Sabbath and honoring His appointed times. She things modern-day Christianity has overlooked many of the verses in both the Tanach ("Old Testament") as well as the New Testament that seem to clearly support these things, and have rather overly focused on certain verses that have been very much taken out of context and misunderstood..!

Despite being of Jewish descent, Jacqueline was rejected from obtaining "citizenship" in Israel, due to her faith in The One True Lord God and Savior Jesus Christ, and for the time being gladly lives in "the nations"- hoping to be of good service to all, Elohim God willing. As a born-again Torah-Keeper, one of her greatest passions is to help expose anti-Semitism, including with relation to Christian history, and encourage Believers in Christ Messiah to be willing to relook at how that may have influenced the doctrines and lifestyle promoted within Christianity today.

All nations whom Thou hast made shall come and worship before Thee, O Adonai; and shall glorify Thy Name.

*Psalm 86:9 *edAKJV, The Holy Bible*

GOD'S NAMES & TITLES USED

There are many references to The Holy Bible in this book and oftentimes God's Hebrew titles and Name is also used. Additionally, as a way to help be protective of His Name, in the way I believe in pronouncing it, sometimes in place of the letter "A" the symbol "-" is used.

I pronounce God's Name as Y-HWEH. I may also refer to Him as Y-H.

The Name Jesus Christ, when using Hebrew, I do pronounce as Y-hoshua Ha'Mashiach. I may also interchange the words Christ and Messiah, which I believe can mean the same thing.

Lastly, there have been many times where the English versions of the Bible have removed God's Name and replaced it with the titles God or Lord. And so if including any of those Scriptures, I have sought to restore His Name to where it originally would have been..!

It is believed that the words "God" and "Lord" are both actually titles, and oftentimes "God" would be translated to the Hebrew word "Elohim," while "Lord" would be translated to the Hebrew word "Adonai."

And to please be clear, I do also believe The Father, Son and Holy Spirit are One and that The Son (Jesus Christ) is Y-HWEH.

ACKNOWLEDGEMENTS

Dr. Richard Schulze and Chris Wark who have both shared, what I believe, to be some incredibly valuable information on detoxification, herbalism, and otherwise.

Paris Hilton, who is seemingly now a top spokesperson against the horrific institutionalized child abuse that has been taking place internationally.

Cathy O'Brien, who has seemingly helped to speak out against "elite" corruption and trauma-based mind control that connects all the way back to what "scientists" did in the nazi holocaust. She has also shared information on writing things out by hand and how she believes it relates to inner-healing.

Mort Fertel, who I believe may have an incredible track record in helping marriages to reconcile that had been struggling and who had found that "marriage counseling" was absolutely not helping them whatsoever.

My "meant to be" husband- whoever he is.

COMING SOON

I've created a free GIFT for my readers that is available NOW and has one of my #1 tips in helping to *discern if he's a narc **from the start**!*

So, I invite you to go to: www.jacquelineservantess.com/from-the-start right now- if you hadn't already- and enter your email address, and I'll send you your free copy without delay!

9 781777 392116